YOUR PLACE IN THE WORLD

Creating a life of vision, purpose, and service.

Marla —
Peace & Blessing on
your Journey —
 Tom
 6-20-10

TOM ANDERSON

Copyright © 2010 Tom Anderson
All rights reserved.

    ISBN: 1439271062
    ISBN-13: 9781439271063
    Library of Congress Control Number: 2009902269

Dedicated with love, affection, and gratitude to all of the many teachers in my life.

Especially to the three from whom I have learned my deepest truths:

to Wesley—my oldest child and only son, who has always represented the deepest calling of soul and who inspired me to take this journey;

to Kate—my daughter and shining light, who represents for me the dawn of new beginnings;

finally, to Leslie—my soul mate and partner on this journey;

...and for caterpillars everywhere.

Sometimes
if you move carefully
through the forest

breathing
like the ones
in the old stories

who could cross
a shimmering bed of dry leaves
without a sound,

you come
to a place
whose only task

is to trouble you
with tiny
but frightening requests

conceived out of nowhere
but in this place
beginning to lead everywhere.

-David Whyte

Prologue

This book began to quietly write itself in me when I was seventeen years old, though it would take more than thirty years to give it a voice within these pages. I remember the exact moment it dropped the first clue into my heart. I was standing on a jetty extending into the Gulf of Mexico in the Florida Keys. My family and I had driven down from our home in central Florida to spend a few days diving and collecting tropical fish for my aquariums. It was a trip we made a few times every year, and it was the kind of vacation I enjoyed immensely.

I was in love with the ocean. I had watched every Jacques Cousteau special on television since I was a child. My idea of a perfect life was one spent on board the Calypso, sailing off to exotic waters in search of adventure. I decided very early I wanted to be a marine biologist when I grew up, and with the time of being grown up fast approaching, I had some decisions to make about my college major and future career path. I had met several people with PhD's in marine biology on our family trips to the Keys, but instead of sailing away to exotic waters, these highly educated young men were working in dive shops and aquarium stores at barely more than minimum wage. It gave my parents pause. They began to suggest more practical college majors for me, ones with a bit more financial stability and a better return on their investment. I reminded them they had always taught me I could be anything I wanted in life, to which they lovingly replied, "Yes, so what you *want* to be is a lawyer—they make good money!"

Which is why I was standing alone on the jetty. I was always a serious kid, at times more so than was good for me, and I had gone off by myself to do some serious thinking. I stood there, the smell of salty water and low tide in my nose. My t-shirt clung to me in the humid air as the setting sun tried to burn the dampness from my skin. A flock of pelicans split the horizon, heading north toward the Everglades and their roost for the night. I watched the scene, feeling it deep in the center of my chest, while turning the question over and over in my mind: *What am I supposed to do?*

In that moment I did something I don't remember ever having done before: I asked for guidance. At the time, I didn't have any spiritual beliefs. In fact, I prided myself on being a scientifically-minded skeptic. But, looking back, I can only describe what happened next as a moment of awakening. After I had exhausted my brain asking the question, *what am I supposed to do*, I finally let it drop down into my heart. I received an answer. It didn't come as words. It came as a feeling, a deep knowing. The answer seemed to come from the ocean herself, but it simultaneously vibrated in my heart. *It doesn't matter what work you do,* the message said, *I will always be here.* What I understood was the ocean wouldn't just be *there*, as in, out *there* on the horizon somewhere, waiting for me. The ocean—with all its beauty, majesty, and mystery—would always be *here*, within my heart.

I turned my back on the ocean that evening, just as the sun set, and walked away from the jetty, satisfied I had received my answer. It would be okay to give up the marine biology dream

Prologue

to pursue something more practical, like business. Soon after, I wrote a poem, the opening lines of which I still remember: *I look to the sea to find myself/ and find the sea is me.* I also wrote an essay about the experience, and both won some local accolades but were soon forgotten. I left for college a few months later, declaring a major in finance and real estate. Saying *no* to marine biology was the right decision, but looking back, I realize I should have asked a few more questions. I should have asked what to say *yes* to.

Twenty-five years went by in less time than the kid on the jetty ever would have believed possible. I left college with a business degree in hand, married, started a family, and developed a successful career in commercial mortgage banking. In those years after college I began setting goals about the perfect professional opportunity, the kind that would offer the elusive mix of challenge and financial security while allowing me to use the skills and talents I treasured the most. Every decision I made seemed to be the responsible and right one at the time, but something was always missing. Lives are built that way, one small decision, one fractional course correction, after another. Then one day we wake up with an ache in the center of our chest and wonder where we went wrong.

My turning point occurred the day my boss walked into my office with some good news. He was ready to make me a partner. It didn't come as a surprise; we had talked about it before, but now he had taken the tangible step of hiring an attorney to draft an agreement. I had a goal of owning my own business for years, but something was wrong. I heard myself telling my boss it was great news but my heart registered nothing. After he left my office, I wondered if he could sense my reservation. I also wondered why, after all the years of working toward this

Your Place in the World

exact goal, when it was finally within reach, I wasn't sure it was what I wanted after all. It was like I had been dating my job for years and was now being offered a marriage, only to discover this was not a place I could spend the rest of my life. Simply put, I felt I was living a life that was just too small.

Unlike the kid on the jetty, as an adult, I had a spiritual practice, and so I began to ask for Divine guidance. I thought about the ache I carried in my chest, the metaphor I used to describe the yearning I often felt. I couldn't understand what I was yearning for because I thought I had everything I could possibly need or want. I was being offered a chance to own a part of an established mortgage company, to fulfill the goal I started formulating all those years ago in business school. Was I just unable to be satisfied?

Guidance showed up this time in the form of an email from a business acquaintance. In it, he mentioned a not-for-profit organization he supported that took people on vision quests. The message got my attention. I loved to camp, so the idea of getting away from my life for nine days in the wilderness appealed. Maybe this was what I needed to do to find some answers, finally put the yearning to rest, and get on with the rest of what promised to be a very successful and prosperous life. And so, I decided to go on a vision quest. My goal was to figure out what I needed to say to my boss about his generous offer. Goals can be funny things; we create them so they might bring some focus and order into our lives only to find they lead us down a new road we never even knew existed before, or perhaps they take us back to an old one we thought we left behind long ago.

This book is the story of my vision quest. It's also an invitation to take one of your own. While you might chose the form I

Prologue

did and go away for nine days in the wilderness, you also might choose to work through the processes I offer in this book in the comfort and convenience of your own hometown. While the book you hold in your hands is my story, what I want you to know is that it is *your* story, as well. Like many good stories, it is filled with unexpected turns, interesting characters, and even a little magic. There is a bit of heroic greatness in the heart and soul of each of us, and you can discover yours for yourself—if you are willing to go on a journey.

Contents

PROLOGUE — vii

ACKNOWLEDGEMENTS — xv

INTRODUCTION — xvii
The call to live a mythic life

CHAPTER 1
MYTH AND THE HERO'S JOURNEY — 1
Seeing our lives as an adventure of discovery
Waking to the Drum. What is Myth? The Hero's Journey. The Hero's Boon
Our Place in the World. Tests along the Way. Spirit, Soul, and Ego.
Ritual and Ceremony. A Journey Home. Activities

CHAPTER 2
DARKNESS ON THE LAND — 31
Finding our vision
My Miasma. Quiet Desperation. Vision. Finding our Vision
A Journey Through Time. The Source of the Desperation. Activities

CHAPTER 3
THE CALLING — 57
Finding our purpose
Peacemaker. Needs, Wants, and Yearnings. The Call to Adventure and the Refusal.
The Soul and our Purpose for Being. Finding our Purpose.
We Can't Do Anything Else. Imaginal Cells. The Response. Activities

CHAPTER 4
SEVERANCE — 89
Serving our people
Everything. The Ending that is a Beginning.
Accumulating Layers vs. Traveling Light. A Guard at the Gate.
Finding our People. Mother Earth, Father Time, and a Daily Practice.
Opening the Door and Stepping Through. Activites

CHAPTER 5
THE THRESHOLD — 115
Claiming what has always been
Solo Time. The Threshold. Fasting, Solitude, and Exposure.
Stating your Name and Stepping Through the Portal. Trouble at the Border.
The Time in the Threshold. Claiming the Boon. Heading for Home. Activites

CHAPTER 6
INCORPORATION — 149
Bringing the boon to our people
Leaving the Wilderness. The Return. Dragons at
the Gate. Bringing the Boon Home.
Creating Forms. Practices. A New Beginning. Activities

EPILOGUE: — 183
Living the mythic life

ADDITIONAL RESOURCES — 189
ABOUT THE AUTHOR — 191
NOTES — 193

Acknowledgements

The writing of this book has been a journey for me, and while it has felt lonely at times, there is no doubt it would never have been completed without the loving support of many people.

I begin every list of the blessings in my life with the name of my wife, Leslie Anderson. Her words of encouragement, her love of me through all we have been through together, and her support of my dream, all contributed, not just to this book, but to the kind of person I am today.

I give thanks for the many spiritual teachers who I have learned from: Rev. Greg Barrett, Rev. Patricia Bass, and Cat Running Elk, among others.

I give thanks to the vision quest guides, Michael Bodkin and Linda Sartor with Rites of Passage. They were there for me at the edge of the threshold and on my return when I needed them most.

I deeply appreciate all of the editorial feedback from Jeanine Fox, Cat Running Elk, Rev. Toni Boehm, Michael Bodkin, and, particularly, Sonita Loyd, who gave an extraordinary amount of time and care to the final editing process.

I acknowledge the presence of God in my life, and give deep thanks for the way God manifests in the wild places of Mother Earth.

Thank you all.

Introduction

The call to live a mythic life

You are a hero and carry within you a gift for your people. This gift is a blessing that can fuel a dream, create an abundant life, and even change the world. We are living in an age, like many before, which could use a few heroes. Perhaps your time has come.

M.E.P. Seligman, who is known as the father of positive psychology, says there are three kinds of life to which human's aspire.[1] The first is a pleasant life, one that is filled with experiences, memories, and emotions that are generally satisfactory and without great turmoil. The second level is the good life. In living the good life, we have mastered the skills needed to provide for our basic necessities. Further, we have discovered our signature strengths and have begun employing them to achieve a sense of achievement in our lives.

But for some, neither the *pleasant* life nor the *good* life is enough. For some, there is a desire for yet another way of living. This third way is the pursuit of meaning, where we are not only

Your Place in the World

deploying our signature strengths, but we are doing so within a framework of serving something larger than ourselves.

It is this level of life I call *the mythic life*, for it is the way of the hero.

The pursuit of the first or second kind of life mentioned above is based on an assumption there is something missing or wrong with our current state of being, there is a void to be filled. The mythic life is based on the opposite belief: there is nothing actually *missing* in ourselves, but there is much to be *discovered* and *shared*.

Joseph Campbell, the mythologist whose books are cited as references throughout this book, taught that myths arose from the collective human soul as a way of expressing the highest ideals to which we could aspire, lighting the way to the possible. For some, myths have become a container within which to place their dreams for safekeeping. As long as they can read stories about heroes or watch them on a screen, they are entertained and perhaps even satisfied for a time living lives of unfulfilled dreams.

This book is a call for you to take the container down off the shelf and begin to live your own personal myth. It is a call to allow your dreams to guide you on a journey of self discovery that will not only change your life, but will change the world as well. We are the heroes whose stories have been told countless times and in countless languages throughout human history. We are the heroes being called forth on a quest, and it is our time to answer the call.

This book was inspired by my own personal vision quest. "Vision quest" is a name early Western-European anthropologists gave to ceremonies they observed being performed by Native American cultures.[2] Perhaps the ceremonies reminded

Introduction: The call to live a mythic life

the anthropologists of their own cultural mythologies about questing knights in search of the Holy Grail. Modern vision quests borrow many of the customs and traditions from the Native American culture and give credit to them for their teachings. Typically, however, the modern version is an amalgam of many cultures and, therefore, does not strictly belong to any particular one.

For the Native American, as well as other indigenous cultures around the world with similar rites, the vision quest is considered to be critical for the development of the participant into a fully adult member of the tribe. The vision quest is important not only for the participant to come to know the self but also for the participant to understand their relationship with their tribe, their world, and the spirit nature they believe resides in all things. Black Elk described several reasons someone might want to "cry for a vision or lament" (his name for the vision quest ceremony) but he said there is one reason, above all others:

> *... perhaps the most important reason for "lamenting" is that it helps us to realize our oneness with all things, to know that all things are our relatives; and then in behalf of all things we pray to Wakan-Tanka that He may give to us knowledge of Him who is the source of all things, yet greater than all things.*[3]

In its broader context, the vision quest is a rite of passage, a way of marking a transition from one phase of life to the next. Campbell identified this innate human desire to experience these rites as indicative of the need to reenact the myth of the hero's journey. In the hero's journey, a version of which has been found throughout time in cultures all over the world, an individual is called forth to retrieve something lost or stolen that is crucial to the life and well-being of their community. While the thing the hero searches for in the myths might be a physical object, it actually represents something else: an idea, a manner of living, or a vision for the world.

How do you know if the time has come to begin your own hero's journey? There are many possibilities, of which these are only a few:

- You have just graduated from high school or college and have no idea what to do next. There seems to be no shortage of good advice being offered, but none of it speaks to your heart. Your whole life is before you, and you are ready to begin—if only you could figure out where to start.
- You are in the middle of your life. You have all the things that are supposed to make you happy: a loving family, plenty of possessions, and a career that does more than just pay the bills. But you are not happy. Every day it seems to get just a little harder to go to a job that no longer inspires you the way it once did, if it ever did at all.
- You have spent your entire life trying to please other people, but something has shifted, and you feel as if you are straining at the seams of your old self. Something new is pushing out from deep inside you, and you want to find out what it is.
- You are dealing with a major life change. Perhaps you have recently experienced the loss of or separation from a loved one, the ending of a job or career, or the passing of a milestone. Maybe this shift has brought you to

Introduction: The call to live a mythic life

reconsider all you have held true, and you have begun to wonder what your life is really all about.
- You have had a level of success in your life but are now feeling an urge to serve in a deeper and more meaningful way. You feel a yearning to give but do not know how to begin.

About now you may be thinking this is another self-help book. You would be partly right, but you would also be partly wrong. This book does ask you to do some things to help yourself, but it is not a manual on how to make a million dollars, manifest a mate, or create a new business. There are plenty of those books out there, and they are fine if that's what you are looking for. I decided to write this book because most of those self-help books are missing an important point. While they may talk about the importance of finding one's life purpose, almost none of them give the reader practical ways to discover their purpose. Additionally, life purpose is framed almost entirely from the perspective of Seligman's first two levels of human aspiration with little attention devoted to the third. This book is meant to not only help you find your purpose in life, but also to understand how you might employ your purpose in the service of a larger vision.

So, here's the disclaimer: While following the steps outlined in this book will ultimately help you live a life of joy, it might also bring about some temporary moments of unhappiness. The hero's journey of self-discovery is not necessarily an easy one. Like all journeys, this one will require you to leave some things behind. There will be a period of wandering in the darkness when you wonder why you ever set foot on this road in the first place.

Your Place in the World

When those dark times come, you might find some solace by remembering the smallest seed begins to put down roots and send up shoots while in the darkness. We are not required to heal all of our wounds before we begin, so feel the fear and walk forward anyway. This is a journey the world needs us to take, and if you have come this far, you are already on the path.

When I returned from my personal vision quest, I decided I wanted to create opportunities for others to have similar experiences without necessarily going into the wilderness for nine days. This book is one of the ways I have attempted to do so. **It is my intention it be read and used as if you are actually on a vision quest, with the focus being on the journey rather than the destination.**

The reflection questions placed in the body of the chapters and the activities at the end of each chapter are an integral part of the vision quest process. The reflection questions are a signal it is time to stop and contemplate what you have just read. The activities at the end of each chapter provide the structure and framework for the processes described in the chapters. By working through the activities, you will be taking your own hero's journey. The reflection questions and activities are meant to assist you in deeply understanding and integrating the ideas in the chapters, so please do not skip them. It is one thing to read about concepts and understand them intellectually; it is another to experience the power of living them.

The questions and activities in the book are intended to provide you with a complete experience, but for a more in-depth process, please visit my website, www.liveamythiclife.com. There

Introduction: The call to live a mythic life

you will find additional resources and downloads to guide you through your hero's journey, including worksheets you might find helpful to use while doing the activities.

Before I left on my vision quest, my wife Leslie gave me a package of cards to take along—one for each day of my trip. The words of encouragement she wrote to me in those cards I now offer to you as a "Letter from Home" at the beginning of Chapters 2-6. While these are notes from my beloved, read them as if they are being written to you personally from your own beloved—a wife, husband, future lover, parent, God, loving universe—whatever form your beloved might take.

The mirror of wild nature can teach and inspire us, so I recommend you spend as much time as possible outdoors as you do the activities. When you venture into the wild, be sure to use safety precautions. Make sure someone knows where you are going and when you will return. Consider taking a friend along. Finding the hero within is meant to be a metaphor, not an invitation to dangerous behavior.

Before beginning Chapter 1, purchase a journal or a notebook to use specifically for this process. Record the answers to the reflection and activity questions in your journal, as well as any other thoughts you have about your journey. Consider taking some time every day while you are reading this book to write in your journal.

I don't know why you have chosen to read this book, but know this: your hero's journey has begun. Your entire life has led you to this moment, this decision, this turning point. You are standing at the edge of a threshold, beyond which nothing will ever be the same.

Campbell describes the beginning of the hero's journey like this:

> *The familiar life horizon has been outgrown; the old concepts, ideals and emotional patterns no longer fit; the time for the passing of a threshold is at hand.*[4]

Maybe your own "time for the passing of a threshold is at hand." If so, I hope this book will serve you as you search for a light to shine into the dark places you see ahead. Life is a rich and beautiful experience when it is lived mythically, and we are meant to do so. We are all heroes. Each of us has a unique and crucial gift to discover within ourselves and bring to the world. I invite you to join me on this journey. Welcome, friend.

Chapter 1

Myth and the Hero's Journey
Seeing our lives as an adventure of discovery

Our lives are the stories of heroes, called forth to find and retrieve something lost or stolen—the hero's boon.

> *I implore you, submit to your own myths.*
> *Any postponement in doing so is a lie.*
>
> *- William Carlos Williams*

Chapter 1

Waking to the Drum

I awoke to the soft but insistent sound of a beating drum. It took a minute for me to remember where I was, but as I opened my eyes and looked around, the cold air on my face reminded me. I was zipped into my sleeping bag, lying on the ground under a small nylon tarp around the edges of which I could see a gray sky just beginning to brighten.

As my mind cleared, I felt a renewed sense of time and place. It was Tuesday, the second morning in base camp, and the start of the fourth day of my vision quest. We had driven deep into the White Mountain wilderness of California two days earlier and had found an amazing spot to set up camp. We were in a canyon that provided everything we needed: a clear running creek for fresh water, room to spread out, and huge boulders stacked one on top of the other, providing protection from the wind and shade from the sun. Today was the day I would leave base camp to begin a three-day period of solitude and fasting—a period constituting the heart of the vision quest.

My companions and I had come to that place in the wilderness in search of answers. Although we each had different needs and desires, we all came because a part of our lives just wasn't working anymore, and we yearned to know where to go next. We had, each in our own way, felt we had lost something, or it had been stolen, and we wanted it back.

The drumming continued and I understood it was coming from one of the guides as a wake-up call. I was being summoned to wake up, not only to the day, but to the rest of my life; I knew I couldn't put it off any longer. I unzipped my bag, quickly put on my clothes in the morning chill, and began to stuff my gear into my backpack in preparation for leaving base camp. Around me, I heard the others doing the same. The drumming had stopped, no one was speaking, and there was a reverential hush in the canyon that implied the importance of the work we were each beginning.

We gathered in the central area of the camp where, for the previous two days, we had sat in council and shared meals. This had been our living room, and we had, for a time, formed a kind of family there. We had all spoken from our hearts, sharing hopes and dreams, joys and sorrows, wins and wounds. We had set our intentions in that space for the solo time ahead, and now it was time to part from one another. The guides led us to a small circle of stones on the ground—our threshold circle. It was about three feet across and consisted of no more than a dozen rocks. I remember looking at it and thinking it was unimpressive. I thought at the time the guides should have built something more elaborate. Little did I know the power a simple circle of stones can hold.

One by one, we were invited to step into the circle. One of the guides waited there for us, one hand holding an abalone shell

Chapter 1: Myth and the Hero's Journey

filled with smoldering sage, cedar, and sweet grass, a feather in the other. One by one, we stepped in to receive a blessing from the guide as we were smudged with the purifying smoke. One by one, we stepped out of the circle, shouldered our packs, and headed off to our solo time in quest of a vision.

As I stepped out of that simple circle, I knew something had already shifted inside me. I had been called on my own journey of self discovery, and the act of walking off alone into the wilderness was proof to me I was already well on my way. In that moment it didn't really matter to me what lay ahead or what vision I might or might not find. I had been anointed, and now I was going off on a quest. I was a hero, and nothing could ever take that from me.

What is Myth?

When I teach a class or lead a workshop about the hero's journey, I often begin by asking the participants what they think of when they hear the word "myth." I get a variety of answers, but they always include things like "fanciful story," "something not true," or "old stories about people who lived a long time ago." It is fairly common to use the word *myth* to imply something is not factual or is based solely on rumor and speculation.

While they may involve fantastical ideas, myths actually speak to truths even greater than mere facts. These old stories resonate for us today because their messages are timeless. They speak through the ages because at their core, they speak of eternal truths. They are not just the stories of ancient people, they are our stories. While myths might involve fanciful plots filled with larger-than-life characters that are hard for our

Your Place in the World

rational minds to believe, at their core these stories are real for us because they speak to our souls.

Perhaps no one has done more to further our understanding of the myths of the world than Joseph Campbell. Fairly late in his life and career, Campbell participated in a series of interviews with Bill Moyers that appeared on PBS called *The Power of Myth*. In the companion book of the same name, Campbell says myth has served four different functions throughout time: a mystical function, a cosmological function, a sociological function, and a function that attempts to explain the meaning of life.[1]

The mystical and cosmological functions are perhaps the oldest, providing our ancestors with a means of understanding their worlds. These functions served to convey the idea of experiencing awe before the transcendent mystery of the universe and then to explain the origins of these great mysteries. Imagine being an early human looking up into a night sky filled with stars and then creating stories reflecting your sense of the awe and wonder at the site. Your children ask you the same kinds of questions children ask today: "Why?" "Why is the sky blue? Why does it rain? Why does the elephant have a long trunk?" and so you create stories to answer their questions. The stories are told and retold, handed down from one generation to the next, becoming part of the culture of future generations.

We have lost some of our relationship with mystery. In our modern age, if we don't have the answer, we at least have a sense the answer can be found and the solution known. Our great scientific advances have convinced us whatever mystery remains in the universe will one day be understood through the power of our intellect. To this I would counter it is the mystery of life that makes it compelling. There is something within us that

Chapter 1: Myth and the Hero's Journey

craves the feeling of awe and wonder as we behold the creative power of a marvelous universe.

The sociological function, which can be thought of as the law and order function, arose as people began to live together in larger communities and to create more complex social structures. Stories were used to pass along important information about morals and codes of conduct, thereby playing an important role in the development of human societies. But the sociological function of myth also has a dark side, for in addition to uniting us, myths can be used to separate us from one another. We can see this happening when we confront a fundamental, literal view of stories, sacred texts, or belief systems. In its mundane forms, the sociological function of myth arises as strict dogma, forced ritual, and subjugation of those who do not share the beliefs of those in positions of power. At its extreme, we have events like those of September 11, 2001, when a small group of people held so radically to their interpretation of their cultural and religious myth they felt justified in committing mass murder in the name of their god.

Finally, myth serves to teach us how to live a human life under any circumstances. This function speaks to us about what it means to be fully alive and engaged in life. This is the personal story function of myth, and it serves to connect us to our souls, to our communities, and to our deeper truths.

When we begin to see myth as a reflection of our own personal stories, we have a means by which to see our lives in a larger context. We can then come to understand our purpose in life and our place in the world. Understood in this light, the story we are reading or seeing enacted on the movie screen, for example, one about a common man heading off into strange lands to find the sword stolen from the castle, becomes our

Your Place in the World

personal story about how we must search for our own identity, our source of connection to our community, our purpose in life. Without a means to understand our own personal stories, we might experience a feeling of hopelessness. Without this connection to our own true natures, we lose sight of the importance of our connection to the wider world and our place in it. My desire is we begin to tell our own story, to reveal the arc of our lives so we might see the direction we are going. It is time that we plumb the depths of our souls so we might find the true beauty and purpose lying there.

Myth can serve to remind us of the deep interconnected relationship we have with each other and the universe and the importance each of us plays in the grand scheme of creation. Native Americans, like other indigenous peoples around the world, understand this relationship, and it can be seen in their myths and the ceremonies they use to remind themselves of the lessons those myths teach. There is an understanding of the need for individual members of the tribe to come to know who they are, what roles they have been born to play on earth, and what gifts they are to bring to their people. In the process of coming to know their own stories, individual members can then see how their lives fit into the greater cosmic story unfolding all around them.

In the Native American version of the vision quest, a young person, after being prepared by an elder in the tribe, goes out into the wilderness for a period of fasting and solitude to find their vision. It is understood this vision is meant to provide a touchstone they can return to any time they begin to lose their

Chapter 1: Myth and the Hero's Journey

way or question who they are and what they have been born to be and do. The vision they seek is also of great importance to the tribe. By finding their purpose, the young person is implicitly finding the way they are meant to serve their community. At this point, they often will take on a new name, one that serves to communicate to anyone they will ever meet the true nature of their soul and the gifts they were born to share.

As you read the rest of this book and work with the reflection questions and activities, I invite you to observe how all four functions of myth are present in your experiences and in your wider life. Be aware of the mystery of life your ancient ancestors might have felt when looking into a night sky. Be like a child and question the source of everything around you. Watch for those moments when the experience of your hero's journey pushes against your previously held ideas about how your life is supposed to function, and ask yourself where those beliefs originated. Finally, as you seek out the traces of your story and begin to find the meaning contained within it, know this experience is universal and you are walking in the steps of countless heroes before you while you pave the way for many more to follow.

The Hero's Journey

Societies are built around shared beliefs, customs, and modes of behavior. An important foundation to the formation of a society is the shared interpretations of stories. This is one way societies identify themselves and separate those who are members from those who are not. We are expected to take on the general beliefs of the society into which we have been born; to do otherwise would threaten its existence.

Your Place in the World

In *The Power of Myth*, Campbell tells us myth is the shared dream of society, and dreams are the private myth of the individual. So long as those two are congruent, the individual can lead a perfectly happy life within the confines of his or her society. If they are not congruent, and the individual attempts to force himself or herself to continue living within the bounds of the public myth, then breakdown will occur. It is at the point where the dream of the individual is out of step with the dream of society that the hero's journey begins.[2]

There is a fine line between breakdown and breakthrough, between those we would try to medicate as neurotics and those we would call prophets, between madness and genius. The difference is not just a matter of degree but also a matter of process. While there is a time and place for doctors, therapists, and psychiatric medications, I wonder sometimes how much creativity we as a culture might be medicating away. Human experience has always included a certain amount of chaos and pain, and it is in the struggle we come to understand the totality of what it means to be human. In our modern society, we have lost touch with the processes indigenous cultures used to help their members navigate the difficult transitions of life.

The hero's journey is a kind of process. It can be seen as stages that occur more or less chronologically. In *The Hero with a Thousand Faces*[3], Campbell describes the phases of the hero's journey and provides examples of how this story line shows up in many cultures throughout time. These stages form the basis of most modern vision quests, and we can find them in our own lives, as well. By looking for them, we can begin to truly experience them and even put them to work on behalf of our personal search for meaning.

Chapter 1: Myth and the Hero's Journey

The traditional story of the hero's journey often begins with a problem or dilemma plaguing the hero or his people, what I call "darkness on the land." Our personal stories might begin in a kind of darkness, as well. Perhaps a job is lost, a major life transition has occurred, or our lives are simply in a state of imbalance. While the light might not have literally gone away from our world, there is a feeling of darkness we can't see a way out of.

While the world is in darkness, something happens that gets the hero's attention. Perhaps a stranger knocks at their door, a new and different path through an otherwise well-known forest is discovered, or a hunted animal is followed into a cave. This is the call to adventure. When your call comes, you have a choice: you can answer it or not. If you answer, you will set off on a new adventure with no clear way of knowing where the journey will lead you. If you ignore it, you might spend the rest of your life dealing with the question, "What if?" Whichever you choose, once you have experienced the call, your life will never be the same again.

Once the call has been heard and answered, the hero enters into a process of severance, eventually leaving behind the world he has previously known. In order to fully engage in the process of the hero's journey, you will need to leave some aspects of your life behind as well. The severance might be temporary, like when you leave your house for the day to do one of the activities in this book and then return that evening. Or, the severance could be permanent, like when you decide to finally let go of a habit or belief that no longer serves you. Either way, a kind of freedom will be found in the process.

As the hero completes his severance, a portal will appear and beckon him to cross. When the hero steps across the portal,

Your Place in the World

he enters into a period of wandering and adventure called the threshold. It is here the hero will be tested. It is in the threshold you will be tested as well, but the testing is not to be feared, for it will provide information for you to use when you return.

Eventually, the hero returns from the threshold, and you will, as well. The final phase on this journey is incorporation. It is here the hero returns to his people with stories to tell and gifts to share. You will leave the threshold and enter into a period where you learn how to bring what you have found there to life so you might serve your people. The incorporation period may mark the end of one journey, but it is truly the beginning of another; the true test of the hero will come when he brings his gifts into the world.

It is important to note, while these phases occur chronologically in the story of the hero's journey and on a vision quest, it is possible we may experience some aspects of each of these phases simultaneously in our lives. For example, we might be in a kind of severance period with a particular relationship, a wandering threshold experience regarding our career, and in an incorporation period regarding childhood memories—all at the same time. The goal of this book, however, is not to identify what phases of the journey we are in, but rather to offer a path where we can immerse ourselves in the process itself.

It is helpful on any journey to have a map, the better to see where you have been and where you wish to go next. The diagram shown on the next page is a map of the hero's journey and will appear throughout the pages ahead to orient you to where you are in the process. You will begin the path at the stone

Chapter 1: Myth and the Hero's Journey

labeled "Darkness on the Land" and move in a clockwise direction around the circle until you arrive at "Incorporation."

There is a reason I have used a circular diagram; this journey is not a once-in-a-lifetime experience. Many mythological stories end with the hero feeling an urge to leave home once again. Eventually, we will feel the haunting of a new kind of imbalance in our lives and, if we are paying attention, will hear the call to a new adventure. We will step through the portal and into the threshold coming out again with new stories to tell and additional gifts to share. Each time through, we prepare ourselves for the last and greatest adventure of them all when we move from this existence into the next.

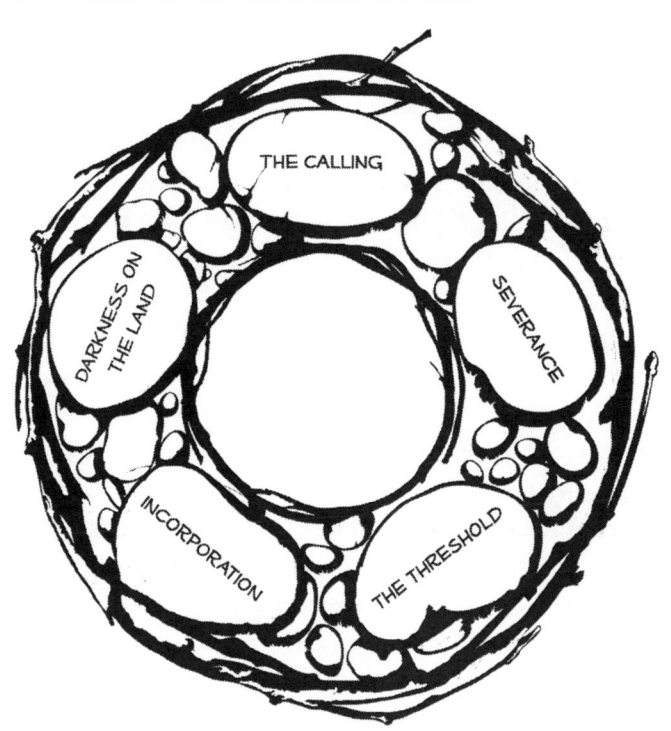

The Hero's Boon

In the myth of the hero's journey, the hero-to-be is called forth to find or retrieve something lost or stolen. Although the hero may or may not actually find the thing he thought he was seeking, he will always find something of great value: the hero's boon.[4] The boon is something that returns the hero and the hero's people to wholeness, to prosperity, and to health. It is a blessing that brings light into darkness and peace to the land. In the myths, the boon might take the form of a religious relic, like the Holy Grail; it might be a weapon with magical powers; or the boon might be a person, such as a princess, who must be returned to her kingdom.

While the hero's boon is something lost or stolen, we might be experiencing its absence as something missing in our lives or in the world. The missing boon sometimes shows up as a feeling of incompleteness or of having possibly made a wrong turn somewhere along life's path. We may feel we are the ones who are lost or a part of ourselves has been stolen. While the mythological hero sets out into the world on a quest to retrieve his boon, our journey will be primarily an inward one.

The boon we seek is a message about how we are meant to live our lives. Once found, the boon guides us in our days and connects us with the world. It points the way to our people and tells us how to serve them. The boon brings meaning to our lives and provides us with strength in our times of struggle. It helps us understand the kind of work we are meant to do and possibly even the place and manner in which we are to do it. Most amazing, the boon to which our souls call us is also the boon the world *needs* us to find. This gift not only leads us to wholeness, it also serves the world.

Chapter 1: Myth and the Hero's Journey

The hero's boon we are seeking on this journey has three parts. Why three parts? The number three has deep archetypal significance for many cultures and spiritual belief systems. In the Christian faith, there is the Holy Trinity of Father, Son, and Holy Spirit. Hinduism has the figure of the Trimurti, which is Sanskrit for "one whole having many parts." In this case, the three parts are Brahma the creator, Vishnu the preserver, and Shiva the destroyer. The number one represents the source from which all else arises, the primal silence within which creation begins. Two is the number of individuation and separation from source, which then sets up a polarity of opposites. Three is the return to unity, the return to source. We naturally divide the world into threes: birth, life, death; past, present, future; morning, noon, night. Three announces wholeness and completion, and connects with mythological archetypes dwelling in our psyches.

The three parts of the boon we seek are vision, purpose, and service. These ideas will be developed further in the coming chapters, but a basic description of each follows:

Vision

A vision, in the broadest sense, is a dream. But it's not just any dream; it is the biggest dream we can imagine for the world. There is a beautiful metaphor for how the universe was originally and is continually being created that says the Great Creator dreamed the universe into existence. Out of nothingness but pure creative thought comes the entirety of everything that is. In this metaphor, the universe continues to dream itself into existence at every moment in time. But where are the dreams held? They are held by every particle in the universe, the human particles and all the other nonhuman particles, as well.

When there is darkness on the land in a myth, the sun has gone away, and in its place, there is death and malaise. Crops won't grow, the people are starving, and no one knows what to do. They are literally and metaphorically "lost in the dark." This is the story of what happens when there is no vision. Into this time of peril, the hero is called to retrieve the light. Finding a vision is a hero's task, and it is the first part of the hero's boon.

Purpose

While our vision is for the world, our purpose, sometimes referred to as a mission, is the specific piece of the world vision we were born to embody. It is through our purpose we deliver our unique gifts into the world in the ways only we can. If vision lies in the ultimate realm of all possibilities, purpose begins to answer the question: "What is *mine* to do?"

The search for purpose is a very common theme in myth. Sometimes it shows up when the main character is of noble blood but has been raised by commoners, and is unaware of his birthright. The character is called on a journey to solve a problem or confront an issue and, along the way, discovers his true identity. Oftentimes the hero must make a journey into the underworld where he consults with the ancestors or other guides and receives a magical tool of great power that imparts additional information about his true identity. In discovering his purpose, the hero uncovers his role in bringing the vision to light. Without the directive power of purpose, vision is unfocused and diffused. Finding our purpose is a hero's task and is the second part of the hero's boon.

Service

The third part of the hero's boon is service. All the hero does must be done in the service of something bigger than himself. Service is the energy that propels the purpose and vision forward. Imbedded in the concept of service is the idea of finding our people, of knowing who or what we are to serve. The power of service binds the hero to his people and provides a reason to make the journey.

A natural tension arises when there is two of anything. Two end points create a line, which cannot stand by itself. With two, there is the tendency to differentiate this from that, us from them. Two implies boundaries and walls. While it might take two to tango, as the saying goes, without the dance, there is no real reason for the two to come together. If the only two parts of the hero's boon we found were vision and purpose, we would feel the tension, as well. Vision calls us to look outward and upward, to look higher to that which unites us. Purpose, on the other hand, is found by looking inward, toward that which differentiates us.

Service is the third part of the boon and as such, resolves the tension between vision and purpose back into a state of unity. Service gives us the greater reason for vision and purpose and provides the energy needed to bring both into tangible form in the world.

In each of the next three chapters, we will look more deeply into these ideas of vision, purpose, and service. In each chapter you will have an opportunity to find one of each of these components of the hero's boon. By the end of the book, you will have collected all three parts of the boon and be ready to return with it to your people. As you read, watch for variations of the diagram below that represents the hero's boon.

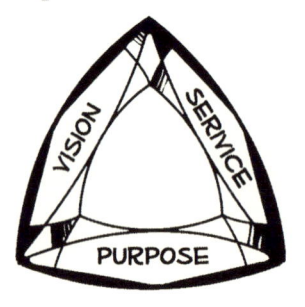

Reflection question: This is a good place to pause and take a moment to reflect on this question: How do you think your life might be different when you find your hero's boon? How do you think the world might be different? Record any thoughts you have about this in your journal.

Our Place in the World

There is a paradox at the heart of the hero's journey: while we are led to take an inner expedition of self-discovery, we are simultaneously called to establish a deeper connection with a wider community. At the intersection between these two paths is where we will find our ultimate place of belonging—our home. When used in this way, home is more than just a physical location and much more than a house. As our house might be the place we return to at the end of the day, home is the place within us and the wider world we can return to at any time to

Chapter 1: Myth and the Hero's Journey

reconnect with who we truly are. When we inhabit this idea of home, we embody an internal connection with our reason for living, as well as a deep and abiding relationship with the outer world around us.

When we find our place in the world we find "our people." When I use this phrase, I am not implying possession of others; I am, instead, referring to our innate need to find connection with other human beings. Our people may or may not be the family or community into which we were born. The journey we take is in part a journey to discover who our people are. We have a symbiotic relationship with our people—we feel served by them and cannot keep from serving them in return. We know we have found our people the same way we know when we have found our place in the world—we will feel as if we have come home.

The idea of the journey home is a common one in myth. One of the best examples of this is Homer's epic poem, *The Odyssey*. In the famous Greek myth, Odysseus, after serving his king for many years in the Trojan Wars, sets out for his homeland of Ithaca. The journey takes ten years and eventually costs the lives of all of Odysseus' men. He faces monsters, angry gods, and terrible storms and temptations along the way. Through it all, it is his yearning for home, powered by the desire to be reunited with his beloved wife, Penelope, which keeps him pushing ahead.

While Odysseus searches for home, aspects of his home are reaching out to him. His son, Telemachus, only days old when Odysseus left to go to war, yearns for his father and sets out to find him. Telemachus is a boy becoming a man without a father to guide him across the threshold. He represents all of the seeds we have sown, which need our attention and our love

Your Place in the World

to reach their maturity. Our search for home is not a selfish act, for there are others who need us to come home just as badly as we need to be there.

Meanwhile, suitors have taken up residence in Odysseus' house, demanding Penelope give up all hope of his return and marry one of them instead. With no other choice, she reluctantly agrees, but only after she has completed weaving a burial shroud for Odysseus' father. Day after day, Penelope sits and weaves the shroud, each night taking apart the rows she has joined. The very fabric of Odysseus' world is coming apart because he is not there. That for which we yearn yearns for us, as well, and will not be complete until we have made our return.

> ***Reflection question:*** *Have you found your "home" and "your people"? If so, how did it feel when you did? If not, how do you imagine it might feel when you do? Spend some time just imagining what your home and your people are like. Imagine as much detail as you can and then write about them in your journal.*

Tests Along the Way

Not all of the challenges Odysseus faced on his journey home were terrible monsters bent on his destruction; some of the most fearsome impediments were beautiful goddesses who wanted him to stay with them on their islands of peace and plenty. How easy it would have been for him to succumb to these temptations and abandon his quest. One simple "yes," and he would spend the rest of his days being sated by beautiful women, his every need and desire attended to in a garden of unearthly delights!

Chapter 1: Myth and the Hero's Journey

For the true hero, however, this would be a fate worse than death. Better to face the unknown, brave the tossing sea, and fight any foe blocking the way than to give up on the dream of all dreams—the return home.

There are so many distractions along our way. We are offered many opportunities to stop and rest, to take an easier path. Sometimes the temptation to do so can be great. We take a job for the financial security it offers in spite of its soul-constricting agenda. We spend nights glued to the television, immersed in the dramas we see there, rather than creating a world for ourselves infused with meaning and purpose.

Who could blame any of us for giving up, for fitting in, for allowing the other voices to have their say? How are we to go about separating the distractions from the goal, anyway? How will we know our home once we see it? Odysseus knew because he had a vision of his home. There were plenty of islands he might have stopped at along the way. Many would have provided all he needed in life and more. But those islands were not his island. He knew, even in those times when he was drugged into a state of stupor and complacency, those homes were not his home.

We can take some guidance from Odysseus in this. Once we come to understand our boon; our vision, purpose, and way of serving; then the temptations and distractions will be obvious. We will be better able to separate those perfectly safe and acceptable ports from the one we were born to sail into. That is not to say we won't still enjoy a few distractions along the way, but when we do, we will have a compass to guide us back to the place we want to be.

Spirit, Soul, and Ego

There are three terms I use throughout this book that have multiple and varied meanings: Spirit, soul, and ego. It is not my intention to provide a comprehensive definition for these, which would take volumes, but it will be useful at this stage for us to come to an understanding of what I mean when I use them.

When I use the word "Spirit," I am referring to the mysterious source from which all arises, as well as the energy that infuses everything. Spirit unites us. You will notice when I use the word Spirit, I capitalize it, because, for me, it is a synonym for God. Other words for Spirit might be the Light, Oneness, the Great Mystery, and the Ground of All Being. There is a sense when we are in touch with Spirit, we are in touch with a transcendent realm of oneness with everything that ever was or ever will be. Spirit represents all we come from and all we have in common. We are all bound to one another, and to the universe, in a sea of Spirit.

When we work with the idea of Spirit in this book, we will be looking outward and upward, but since Spirit is everywhere, this is simply a metaphor for the idea that Spirit lies beyond the mundane of everyday life, even while it is present within every detail of all that is. In this way, I relate Spirit to vision, as they both deal with the idea of the transcendent big picture. We look outward to the world for our vision in the same manner we raise up our eyes to the penultimate to connect with Spirit.

When I use the word "soul," I am referring to the part of us that is the individuated aspect of Spirit. While Spirit is the Ground of All Being, soul is the place of becoming, the manner in which Spirit becomes each of us. Soul represents our core nature, the essence of who we are and have come to be.

Chapter 1: Myth and the Hero's Journey

When I talk about soul, I am implying there is an essential idea, gift, or message we have been born to express, and it is found in the soul.

While Spirit calls us to look outward and upward, soul invites an inward journey. Again, this is a metaphor and not intended to imply that soul is located in a physical place in our bodies. A journey to soul is often represented in myth as a descent into the underworld or a passage through a wild and dark forest. While we can picture Spirit as pure white light, free of earthly bounds, soul can be thought of as dark, mysterious, and earthy.

There is a poem by the Sufi mystic, Rumi, which speaks to this relationship between Spirit and soul:

> *God picks up the reed flute world and blows.*
> *Each note is a need coming through each of us,*
> *A passion,*
> *A longing-pain.*
> *Remember the lips*
> *Where the wind-breath originated,*
> *And let your note be clear.*
> *Don't try to end it.*
> *Be your note.*

In this poem, Rumi depicts Spirit, called God here, as the source of the music, but without the flute, the individuated soul of us, there is no note. In this way, Spirit and soul need one another in order to express in the world. "Remember the lips," is a reminder not to forget our source. "Be your note," is a request our soul cannot ignore.

Ego is the third term I use we need to look at. The term is closely associated with the work of Sigmund Freud, who founded the psychoanalytic school of psychology. In very simplified terms, the ego is the part of the subconscious mind engaged in interacting with the world.[5] Ego has come to mean a lot of things in its general usage, most of which are not very complimentary, but my usage of the word simply means the part of ourselves that ordinarily shows up in our daily lives. In this context, ego is neither good nor bad; it is simply a function of being human. In essence, ego is our personality.

Our ego is a function of two general kinds of influences: our personal experiences, and, to a very large degree, the influences of our culture. When we have an experience of some kind, our ego does two things; it interprets it based on previous similar experiences, and it stores it away to be used to interpret future experiences. The particular culture we live in has a huge influence on our egos, as well. We are constantly being given information and feedback from the people around us about the meaning of events and circumstances in our lives, which our ego then uses to reach its own conclusions.

There is a joke that goes like this: "To a child with a hammer, the entire world's a nail." The ego part of us is the child. The hammer represents the accumulated knowledge we have about the world we live in. The nail represents any kind of life experience we might encounter. When we get new information about our lives and the world, we add another tool to our toolkit. The kinds of tools we get will, in a large part, depend on the kind of experiences we have and the culture we live in. Think about how different a toolkit would look for someone living today in an American city versus someone living in

Sub-Saharan Africa, or ancient Greece. By simply reading this book, you are adding another tool to your toolkit.

If we live in a culture that encourages us to engage with our soul, then we will have an ego that is reflective of our soul nature. Likewise, if we grow up in a culture that is constantly reminding us of our connection to Spirit, then our ego will be more likely to exhibit the qualities of Spirit. Conversely, if our cultural influences are materialistic, then our ego will tend to be so, as well. We can influence and even change our egos over time through a variety of methods. In this book we will begin to influence and transform our egos by looking into the ideas of soul and Spirit as we talk about purpose and vision. We will also begin to bring our egos into the service of something bigger than ourselves as we find the way we are meant to serve in the world.

Spirit and soul are both timeless and unchangeable, but ego is not, and will, in a healthy person, develop and mature over time. While our ego is learning about a constantly changing world, Spirit is calling to us from a still, quiet place, telling us to look higher for our true vision. Simultaneously, soul is inviting us to go inward to find the true purpose of our being, free from the expectations of the larger world. The intention of this book and the work I invite you to do is not to get rid of the ego but to infuse it with a deeper knowledge of your connection with Spirit and the gifts of your soul.

Ritual and Ceremony

The vision quest is a ceremony that reenacts the myth of the hero's journey. The process we are stepping into as we do the work outlined in this book can be a kind of ceremony, as well.

Your Place in the World

Before we move forward, let's take a look more closely at the concept of ritual and ceremony.

Rituals, which are typically done on a regular basis, and ceremonies, which are generally used to mark special occasions are, on a certain level, reenactments of our myths. By reenacting our myths, rituals and ceremonies serve to connect us with their deeper meaning and ground the ideas in our bodies. When candles are lit in a Christian church on Christmas Eve, there is a connection to a very old myth about light returning to the darkness. Whether the light symbolizes the birth of Jesus or an even older story about the lengthening of the days following the winter solstice, those in attendance are reminded light always prevails over the dark.

I have a very simple ritual I use to mark the beginning and ending of each day. Every morning, I stand in front of my kitchen sink with the water just barely trickling out. I hold a small earthenware bowl that was a gift to me from one of my teachers. As the water runs, I take deep breaths and allow my body to relax. I imagine the water represents the good the universe is waiting to give me in the coming day, the blessings that are mine to claim. I see the running water as representing the flow of life, the living waters of Spirit flowing within all things and giving me life and vitality. When I feel I am ready, I move my bowl under the tap and allow it to be filled. I whisper a word or two of thanks, take a sip from the bowl to signify the incorporation of this blessing into my being, and then place it on an altar area in my home where it stays throughout the day.

When my day is done, I take the bowl of water out onto the deck of my house. I hold it reverently in both hands and again relax into the moment. I give thanks for the day, for all of the people in my life, and all of my blessings. I declare the day is

Chapter 1: Myth and the Hero's Journey

done and all is well with my world. I take a small sip to remind me the goodness is always with me and then pour the water on the ground, returning it to the source from which it came.[6]

Small rituals performed simply throughout the day serve to slow us down and raise our awareness and consciousness of the world around us. If we are feeling overwhelmed by the pace of our lives, simply inserting a few rituals into our routine will go a long way toward alleviating the feeling. We have lost so many of the rituals and ceremonies that connect us with one another and with the earth. We can begin to mend the rift one step at a time and, in the process, come to know ourselves more deeply.

Our ancestors understood the importance of ceremony. They marked every change of season, every life's passage, every significant event with some kind of ceremony. Should we do no less to send the hero on his or her journey? The form is not nearly as important as the meaning we bring to it. If it begins to feel rote, it might be time to replace it with something new or to spend some time thinking about its origin.

The process we will walk through in the following chapters is a ceremony that is simultaneously mystical, cosmological, sociological, and soul connected. Through walking this path, we experience the myth of the hero's journey as a rite of passage. By experiencing the stages of severance, threshold, and incorporation, we reconnect to the passages made by so many who have come before us, and we can come to see our lives as a heroic journey to find our boon.

A Journey Home

We are all heroes on our way home. It is a difficult path, but we can take heart in knowing it has been walked by many before us. Their names have been spoken around campfires and written in books. Their deeds have been told and retold countless times and in countless places around the world. Their story is always the same: a man or woman, just like you or me, is called to take a journey to find something of great value for their people. It is time to begin.

Chapter 1: Myth and the Hero's Journey

Activities

1. This activity is intended to deepen your understanding about the hero's journey.

   Bring to mind a story you are familiar with that you think of as being a retelling of the hero's journey. It might be a work of literature, a children's story, or a popular movie. Now, think about the following questions, recording your answers in your journal if you wish:

   - What is the name of the story?
   - Who was the hero (or heroine)?
   - What form did the "Darkness on the Land" take in this story?
   - How did the hero experience "The Calling?" Did the hero answer the call immediately or was there a refusal at first? In either case, what happened next?
   - Was there a moment of "Severance" in the story? What happened?
   - What was "The Threshold" like for the hero? Did they face any monsters, temptations, or distractions (literal and/or metaphorical) in the threshold?
   - How did the hero experience "The Incorporation?"
   - How was the hero different or changed from the start of the story compared to the end of the story?
   - What is your favorite part of the story? Why?

2. Try the following activity if you are interested in bringing more ritual into your life. This exercise is a good way to prepare for some of the activities in the following chapters.

   Think about one small part of your daily life and how you might create a simple ritual around it. It might be the way you wake up in the morning, eat your lunch at noon, or go to sleep at the end of the day. How could you mark this daily occurrence in a manner that honors it and connects you with it in a deeper way? Create a ritual and practice it daily for two weeks. Then make some notes in your journal about any subtle effects it has had on your life.

For additional resources, including free downloadable worksheets you might find helpful in completing these activities, please visit www.liveamythiclife.com.

Chapter 2

Darkness On The Land
Finding our vision

Our story begins, as so many do, with a discordance; the light has gone away. There is a sense something is missing, and until it is found and returned to its rightful place, darkness will prevail.

> *Our desires presage the capacities within us;*
> *they are harbingers of what we shall be able to*
> *accomplish...We are attracted to what*
> *is already ours in secret...Just trust yourself, then*
> *you will know how to live.*
>
> *-Goethe*

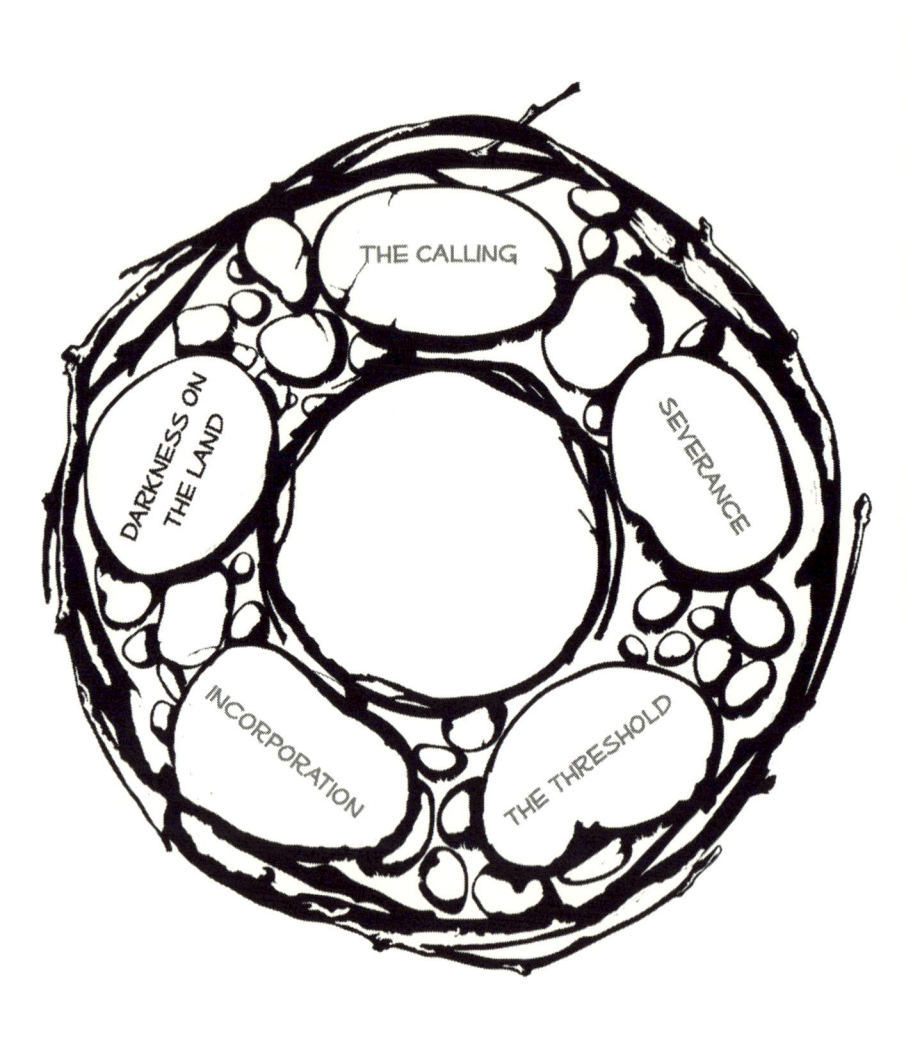

- THE CALLING
- SEVERANCE
- THE THRESHOLD
- INCORPORATION
- DARKNESS ON THE LAND

Chapter 2

Letter from Home: Be joy filled and don't worry—you are perfect just as Spirit created you. I'm thinking of you and believing in you. Can you feel it?

My Miasma

I had a dream. In the dream I am sitting in a small diner. The diner is somewhere in the desert, on the edge of nowhere, but it looks like the kind of place you might find anywhere. People are coming and going in the diner, stopping in for their morning coffee and connecting with the local community. Although the place has seen better days, it has an energy that brings a sense of hope and belonging to those who come through its doors.

In my dream, I am sitting across a table from a man. He is tall and strong, but he has been broken by an existence of unfulfilled wishes and dreams. He is about my age, mid-forties, but he looks much older, having aged rapidly through a life of hard work and difficult circumstances. He has large hands, knotted and calloused from many years of physical labor, and needs a haircut and a shave. The man's eyes have a haunted, empty quality. He is drinking black coffee and seems to be hung-over from too much alcohol the night before.

Your Place in the World

I understand I am supposed to go to work with the man that morning. He has gotten a job that will be hard labor but will pay well. He had some others lined up to help, but they have abandoned him. It is not the first time the man has been abandoned; it happens so often he has come to expect it. Although he has taken orders from others for most of his life, today the man gets to be the boss, and he seems to like the idea of being in charge.

There is a small flicker of hope in the man, but it is a hope born of habit rather than optimism. The man continues to hope for a better life, for respect, for purpose, because to do otherwise would be to lie down and die—and he is not yet ready to die.

A waitress in the diner seems to know the man. Her gaze lingers on him when she stops by the table to refill our coffee cups. She doesn't notice me at all. She stands a few feet away from the table and throws small bits of paper at him, trying to get his attention. When he continues to ignore her, she gives up, sighing deeply, and goes on to serve the other people in the diner.

While we are sitting there, a group of men wearing straw cowboy hats and work clothes come to an open window beside us, and one of them reaches through, nearly touching my shoulder. I look into this new man's face and see the same sense of despair mixed with pride I have been seeing in the man with whom I am sitting. I am not sure if the man at the window is begging for a handout or asking for work, and I wait for the man across from me at the table to respond, but he just continues to stare into his coffee cup. Finally, I shake my head no, and the men in the work clothes and straw cowboy hats angrily leave. In my dream, I feel a little afraid of what they might do next, but they climb into a truck and leave the parking lot.

Chapter 2: Darkness On The Land

A short while later, the man and I leave the diner and get into the cab of his old pickup truck. I feel a little afraid to ride with him, as he seems to still be slightly drunk, but I am even more afraid to say anything about it. We set out for the day's work awaiting us, and as we do, the man speaks for the first time: "Miasma," he says, gesturing with a sweeping motion of his hand at the scene around us, "my miasma." It seems like a strange word for this man to use, but it perfectly describes the scene of desolation and despair I see before me through the windshield of the truck as the two of us ride off to work for the day.

Quiet Desperation

When I awoke from the dream I knew it had something profound to teach me, so I immediately began to write it down. Although I was familiar with the word miasma, I wasn't entirely sure what it meant, so the next day I looked it up and I learned it has two relevant meanings:

> *A vaporous exhalation formerly believed to cause disease, and An influence or atmosphere that tends to deplete or corrupt.*

These two definitions imply a reciprocal relationship between the individual (the one making the vaporous exhalation) and the atmosphere (that tends to corrupt). It might be easy to blame outside influences for the conditions the man in my dream was experiencing, but he was not an innocent victim. While the man was certainly a product of his environment, he was also just as certainly contributing to his situation by his own choices and his assumptions and attitudes about his life. The scene he surveyed through the windshield of his truck was as much a product of his thoughts as anything else. How differently might the scene have unfolded if the man had noticed the waitress or the man wearing the cowboy hat at the window? What if he was awake enough to appreciate the sense of community around him in the diner? We create our own reality through the power of our minds and by deciding where to place our attention.

I write these words at the end of a decade that started with the devastating events of September 11, 2001 and concluded with what has come to be called The Great Recession. One of the things these two bookends to the decade have in common is they have, each in their own way, pushed many of us to ask ourselves some difficult questions: What do I truly value? What is the deeper meaning of my life? What legacy do I want to leave for my children? Sometimes those who are called to ask themselves these kinds of questions lack a framework within which to find the answers, and so the questions are stuffed down with an intention to return to them later. Once asked, however, the questions remain, coming back now and then to haunt our dreams.

Sometimes the people who come to my workshops and retreats are there because their lives have fallen apart in some way: they have lost a job, their family relationships aren't working, or they are lonely and in search of connection with a community. But more often than not, the people who I see are the ones whose lives are pretty much ok. They have a job, loving relationships, and are making meaningful contributions to their communities, but something is still not right. They are feeling a yearning for "something," but cannot determine just what that "something" is.

This human experience of yearning is nothing new. More than 150 years ago, Henry David Thoreau wrote these words: "The mass of men lead lives of quiet desperation,"[1] and in spite of all our progress, it is still true today. My miasma was not unique. For every person who is asking themselves difficult questions about their lives, there are countless others who, in spite of having a very good life, are haunted by dreams of another way of living. I believe it is time for us to listen to this yearning. It is time to question the source of this quiet desperation and begin to explore our souls with the intention of discovering the unique gifts we hold within.

I also believe the sense of yearning we are feeling is coming not just from within us but from the soul of the earth, as well. The earth is desperate for us to wake up to our own deeper meaning and purpose. The world cries out for our true gifts, and our souls answer through the yearning we feel for something else, something different than the story we have been telling as individuals and as a society.

There was a time in my life when my own sense of quiet desperation manifested in what I then described as a persistent ache in my chest. I was feeling a yearning to live a different kind of life based on bringing my most essential gifts into the world, but I had no idea how to go about making that happen. In the beginning, I thought it was all about finding the kind of work I was meant to do. Work is an important aspect of most of our lives because we spend such a large part of our waking hours dedicated to it. But having work to do didn't change much for the man in my dream. He was still living in a state of miasma. Something else was missing.

> **Reflection question:** Are you experiencing something like a sense of "quiet desperation," or a yearning for something you can't quite name? If so, spend a few minutes in silence allowing the feeling to arise. Just be aware of it. Write about the feeling in your journal. Then, give thanks for it, knowing it has come to serve you.

Vision

As I reflected on my dream, I began to wonder what exactly was missing from this man's life. I understood all of the characters in my dream represented aspects of me, reflections of various parts of my psyche. If that were so, then what did the man I was sitting with represent? What was it that was contributing to his (my) state of miasma?

If we look at my dream through the lens of the hero's journey, we can see there is present the kind of "darkness on the land" so many myths begin with. The man cannot see the beauty in the world around him: the waitress, the men at the window, or the community in the diner. He is in a kind of darkness where all he can see is desolation and despair. If the light is to be returned to his world, if the quiet desperation is to be quelled, then the hero's boon must be found and returned to the land—and the first part of the boon is vision.

I introduced the idea of vision in Chapter 1 by suggesting our vision is the biggest dream we can have for the world. When we find our vision, we have found our own personal version of "heaven on earth." Vision comes to us on the voice of Spirit, calling us to look higher, beyond the details of our daily lives to see what is truly possible in the world.

Chapter 2: Darkness On The Land

Since we all have different perspectives and life experiences, we all have different visions. Do you remember the story of the three blind men, each touching a different part of an elephant and thinking through their limited perspective they know what an elephant is? This story describes how we each come to understand our vision, as well. When we describe our vision, we are attempting to describe what is ultimately indescribable. Our vision calls us to look outward into the world, or even the universe, but when we do so, we will always be catching only a small part of the whole.

Vision is the first part of the boon because without it, nothing else makes sense. It is a normal response when things don't seem to be working in our lives or our world to begin rearranging parts of it with the hope that doing so will make a difference. So we change jobs, buy a new house, or leave our spouses in an attempt to shake the malaise we are feeling. But without first having a vision for our lives, for the kind of world we want to live in, how can we even begin to make decisions about what needs to stay and what needs to leave?

A true vision has three characteristics: it inspires us, it stretches us, and it unites us. Think for a moment about those people from history we call visionaries. For me, people like Moses, President John F. Kennedy, and Dr. Martin Luther King, Jr. come to mind. What all three of these men had in common was a powerful and compelling vision for the future. Moses had a vision of a home land for the Hebrew people. Among other things, President Kennedy set forth the vision of landing a man on the moon and bringing him back safely. Dr. King had a vision of people of all colors living together in harmony. Each of these visions inspired others to action, encouraged people to

Your Place in the World

push beyond what they may have previously believed possible, and united many people behind a common cause.

The word *inspire* is made up of the Latin roots *in* and *spirare,* the latter meaning "to breathe." To inspire is to infuse with life and vitality and is therefore the opposite of miasma. When we are inspired, we are given new life. The vision Moses received from God at the burning bush, freedom for the Hebrew people, inspired him and thousands of others to set out on a difficult and dangerous journey without any real sense of where it might take them. A vision infuses us with the life and vitality needed to look beyond what we previously believed to be possible, to boldly step into an uncertain future, and to commit our lives to bringing about its creation.

A powerful vision stretches us beyond our comfort zone. While a vision is something we can absolutely believe in, if we can see exactly how to make it real, then it isn't big enough. When President Kennedy shared his vision of landing a man on the moon, no one on earth knew exactly how to do that. There is mystery in a powerful vision. It is like a path in the woods that curves up ahead so we can't see exactly where it leads, yet we feel compelled to walk it anyway just to see where it takes us. A vision pushes us beyond the comfort zone of our previous successes to dance on the very edge of possibility and discover new ways of living in the world.

While everyone will not share it and some may even hate us for expressing it, a vision has the power to unite people. Dr. King's dream is an example of this aspect of vision. It stirred such venomous animosity among some it eventually cost him his life, but his vision of equal rights for all inspired thousands to take to the streets in a show of unity among the races not previously seen in the United States. When we discover our

Chapter 2: Darkness On The Land

vision, we will have no way of knowing just how it will be received in the world, nor should we care. We simply express it because we know it is true for us. Do not be surprised however, if others begin to show support for your vision once you have shared it, for once expressed, your vision is no longer yours; it belongs to everyone.

Do not think for a moment your vision isn't big enough for the world, for the world has no vision without the contribution of each of ours. The greater collective vision of the world is held in the hearts and souls of men and women everywhere. Together, the visions of today are building the world of tomorrow, and so, without yours, the world will not be complete.

> *Reflection question:* *Spend a few minutes simply sitting quietly while allowing someone you consider to be a visionary to come to your mind. Think about their life, their work, their vision—whatever comes to your mind about them. Record anything that deeply moves you about this experience in your journal.*

Finding our Vision

So, how do we go about finding our vision? There are many instances of heroes having mystical experiences in which they receive a vision of one kind or another. You might be familiar with stories of mystics and saints receiving visions that included thunder and lightning and all kinds of drama, but a vision can also come to us in the most unlikely of circumstances and in the most gentle of manners.

Your Place in the World

One place to begin is with the visionary you thought of in the previous reflection question. While we are in search of our own vision, not a copy of someone else's, the kind of visionaries we are drawn to can give us clues about our personal vision. Powerful visions have a resonate quality about them. Like a plucked string on a guitar will cause another string tuned alike to vibrate, a vision of another that is related to ours will cause a vibration to occur within us. By paying attention to this vibration, we can begin to get clues about the vision we hold deep within us for the world. Another place to look for our vision is in the daily newspaper. The news tends to supply information about what is lacking in the world. When we read the newspaper or watch the evening news on television, we will often see reports about places in the world where things like food, peace, or adequate education for children is lacking. What kind of stories seem to regularly get your attention? Are they the ones about children? If so, what specific kinds of children's stories? Are they the ones dealing with children's health, their education, or the lack of safe homes? These are all clues about how you personally perceive the "darkness on the land."

If the news stories getting our attention tend to be focused on what is missing in the world, it is our vision that provides the answer. If we are drawn to the issue of lack of nutritious food for children, then maybe our vision is of a world where every child is fed. If we are drawn to the issue of conflicts in the world, then maybe our vision is for a world at peace or one where all people can communicate from the heart. When looking for our vision, we are looking for the bigger picture behind the issue at hand. Remember, your vision is the biggest dream you can have for the world; so as you work with these ideas, imagine you are stepping further and further back from the issue until you reach the limits of your imagination.

Our vision for the world will be influenced by our perspective. We can use my dream to illustrate this point. Here are some possible interpretations of my dream from several different perspectives:

- The man is an alcoholic who has created a wasteland of his life because of his addiction. The dream for the world is for sobriety and freedom from addictions of all kinds for all people.
- The man has difficulty communicating. The dream for the world is one of greater communication between people everywhere.
- The dream is about the gap between men and women. The waitress represents women everywhere who are unable to get the attention and rights they deserve from a male-dominated society. The dream is for a world of equal rights for both sexes.

There are many possibilities, but these three examples serve to make this point: depending on one's perspective, a number of different visions could be seen in the same set of circumstances, facts, and details. This would apply whether we are talking about interpreting a dream, sorting through news reports, or thinking about visionaries. We can all look at the same situations and come away with a different idea about our vision for the world.

Finally, our vision for the world will be found, not just by looking into the light, but by turning and facing the darkness or the challenges we have faced in life, as well. Here is a story that illustrates this point. Joseph M. Marshall III, a Lakota elder, tells in his book *Walking with Grandfather*[2] about the origin of the name of his particular tribe. In the old days, before the time of horses, his ancestors were traveling across the prairie when they heard a cry from the back of the procession. The people all turned around and saw that a fire was raging behind them, and it was quickly moving their way. Everyone dropped their few belongings, gathered up their children and the old, and began to run away from the fire. It was no use, however, for it quickly became evident the fire was moving toward them at a much greater rate of speed than they were capable of running. All seemed lost.

Then, an old woman cried out, "We must run into the fire!" Some immediately saw the wisdom in this tactic and began to wrap their children and themselves in wet blankets for protection from the flames. Others refused; they were so deep in their fear they could not see safety could be found beyond the wall of fire, on the ground already burned. Those people died a terrible death. For those who ran through the flames, some died as well, for their lungs simply couldn't stand the heat of the inferno. But many more lived. Those who lived carried scars on their arms and legs from the fire, and they had a new name to always remind them of the gift that facing the fire had brought: Sicangu Oyate, the Burnt Thigh People.

There are plenty of examples of flames around us. There are the larger problems facing us all, and there are the ones we each deal with in our personal lives. We have a choice: we can focus on the flames, or we can look to the possibilities lying beyond them. A powerful vision can get us there.

> *Reflection question:* At this point in your journey, what do you think it might mean to live a life of vision?

Chapter 2: Darkness On The Land

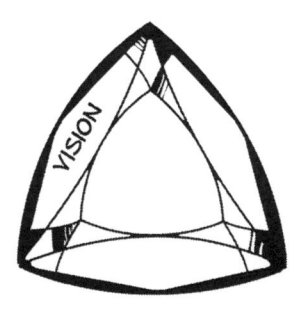

A Journey through Time[3]

Our first human ancestors appeared on the earth around 250,000 years ago. For the next 175,000 years they spent most of their energy just trying to live from one day to the next. Life was hard, and there very likely were times when the future of the human race was in doubt. This was the age of survival.

Around 25,000 years ago, our forbears began to join together in small groups and develop an early form of language, thereby increasing their chances of survival. They started to notice the cycles of nature and created practices meant to placate the unseen forces they believed lay behind those cycles. This was the age of magic.

Around 7,000 years ago, warlords began to arise among our ancestors. It was a time of bloody conflict, and the beginning of slavery. It was an age of conquest and subjugation. This was the age of power.

A new age came up from the chaos about 2,500 years ago. The first laws and codes of conduct began to appear and nation states arose. Societies were more peaceful and ordered, but there was no such thing as individual rights, and most lives were controlled by the power of monarchy and the church. Still, life improved for many. This was the age of law and order.

The next age occurred between 200 and 500 years ago. This was the time of the first scientists—Galileo, Copernicus, da Vinci, and others—who began to question the proclamations of the church and state, thereby challenging the existing structures of their day. The earth, it was discovered, is not the center of the universe and, not only that, is round, not flat. Many wondered: if the church could be wrong about some things, then about what else might the church be wrong? What else might be changed or overturned? Over time, the idea of government by the governed began to emerge, and the American and French revolutions resulted. This was the age of progress.

Our current age began to arise around 150 years ago. This age has seen the end of slavery and the beginning of the Industrial Revolution. This time began with Thoreau's quiet desperation and with Emerson and others who began to see divinity in all things. This new consciousness brought about a greater awareness of the rights of *all* people to live together in peace and prosperity, no matter their color or gender. This age saw the rise of service organizations and human rights groups, plurality and inclusiveness, ecology, and the Internet. In this age there is still much to be done in the areas of civil rights, the environment, and tolerance, but work is underway. This is the age of inclusion.

As humans, we carry the broad sweep of this story within us. Somewhere inside, we remember what it meant to forage for food and try to survive to live another day. We still have the capacity to look with awe and wonder into a clear night sky filled with magic. We know the way to use power, and we understand how it can be abused. We respect law and order,

Chapter 2: Darkness On The Land

and there are times in our lives when we crave it. But we also have witnessed the abuses of rules and regulations and the stagnation that can occur when the letter of the law is held to be higher than its spirit. We have the memory within us, even if we don't have the actual experience in our life, of breaking away from restrictive laws and rules and creating something new for ourselves, just as the founding fathers and mothers of the United States did with their revolution. And, at least on some level, we understand there is value in inclusiveness—everyone deserves to live a life fully realized and complete.

Each of the ages described was shorter than the one that preceded it. What at one time took thousands of years to occur, then multiple generations, is now happening in a lifetime or less. Think about the world our grandparents came of age in and the one our parents were born into. What changes have we seen in our own lifetimes, and what kind of age (or ages) will our children and grandchildren experience?

With each ensuing age in this 250,000 year old story, life has become more complex and, many would argue, more beautiful, but the movement from one age to the next is fraught with challenges. Imagine what it must have been like for those who were living at the dawning of each new age when the stress of letting go of the past and the fear of an unknown future were most intense. What must it have felt like to be one of those individuals who were gradually becoming aware of aspects about their age that simply were not working anymore?

Those who hold a vision for a future different than the present reality have often been derided in their time as being nothing more than dreamers, but the ability to dream of a brighter future in spite of the current darkness has always been the attribute that makes us most human. Our intellects and imaginations allow us to see beyond the current time, to imagine conditions we may not have experienced directly, and to find ways to bring those visions of the future into being. When the times are darkest and all we have is a vision of a future in the light, we have enough to see us through.

> *Reflection question:* Think about two or three particularly difficult or challenging times in your life. What did you learn from each occurrence? Think about these times from the perspective of an evolutionary process. Can you see how various challenges have helped you to grow and evolve into a more complex and more beautiful being? Take some time to write in your journal about this.

The Source of the Desperation

The world is in need of a new vision; one that inspires us, stretches us, and unites us, but we can't wait for someone else to come along to offer us their dream to follow. Time is moving much too fast. The next age will come whether we are ready for it or not. We have the power and the responsibility to dream the next age into being, to vision it into reality.

In 1984, in his ground-breaking book, *Megatrends*, John Naisbitt wrote, "We are living in the time of the parenthesis, the time between eras," and in spite of the passage of nearly thirty years, it feels as if we are still in a time of transition. Naisbitt went on to say this is a "great and yeasty time, filled with opportunity," but we will need "a clear sense, a clear conception, a clear vision of the road ahead" in order to make it safely to the other side.[4]

Chapter 2: Darkness On The Land

The responsibility of leadership in the next phase of our human history lies with each of us. The age of inclusion is still young and we are still learning that along with the privilege of great freedom comes the responsibility of leadership. The vision for tomorrow will come from the collective vision of each and every one of us. We cannot expect another to provide a vision for us to follow; we must find our own.

What if the purpose of the quiet desperation is to reawaken all the knowledge of the ages stored within us, to tap into the potentials already existing in fragmented forms, and to assimilate them into something new, something unlike any age we have experienced before? If we are to live a mythic life, we may very well need some magic as well as power. We will need law and order balanced by the progress of the individual. We will need inclusion in a form that recognizes the value of all phases of our story.

We have a choice; we can live in a state of miasma and desperation, or we can begin a journey of assimilation. Our individual paths in life are paths toward wholeness and completion. Isn't it a beautiful thing that what we each crave is also what the world needs most?

There is a paradox at work here: While our search for the source of our sense of desperation is self-serving, it is not strictly a self-centered process. Simply coming to know ourselves better will not be enough; we must also reach an understanding of how we fit into the world and how we are to serve it. As we come to understand our vision, we will also come to see how we are bound to the earth. Is it any wonder we are feeling this inner yearning at a time when the earth so desperately needs us to find a deeper understanding about how we are all connected?

Your Place in the World

As we dig deeper within our own souls, we also come to see the wider relationship we are in with the great oneness of Spirit. As we come to know the part, we come to know the whole. Our own sense of quiet desperation, the darkness on our land, is a sign we will soon be called to discover our gifts and bring them into the world.

Activities

These activities are designed to help you uncover clues about your vision. Do at least one of these before moving on to the next chapter.

At this stage, you are looking for clues, not final answers, although you may discover those, as well. Don't be concerned if the clues you find here don't make much sense to you. We will work to make sense of the clues in the Incorporation phase of your journey.

If you have difficulty with doing these activities, go back and reread the section in the chapter titled *Finding our Vision*. You might also want to visit www.liveamythiclife.com where you will find worksheets you can download to use for these activities.

1. This activity will help you find where your vision resonates with the vision of others. There are several steps, but the entire activity can be completed in an hour and is best completed in one sitting. This activity relates back to the following idea from the chapter:

    Powerful visions have a resonate quality about them. Like a plucked string on a guitar will cause another string tuned alike to vibrate, a vision of another that is related to ours will cause a vibration to occur within us. By paying attention to this vibration, we can begin to get clues about the vision we hold deep within us for the world.

Step One: Turn to a clean page in your journal and create a table that looks like this:

Visionary	This was/is their vision	Attributes of their vision

Step Two: Sit quietly for a moment and allow the name of someone you consider to be a visionary to come into your mind. This might be the same person you thought of during the Reflection Question in this chapter, or someone new. Write their name in the left column under the heading "Visionary."

In the middle column, under the heading "This was/is their vision," briefly describe what their vision was.

Now, go to the third column and under the heading "Attributes of their vision," begin to write down whatever comes to your mind when you ask yourself the following questions:

- How did this visionary's vision inspire people?
- How did their vision stretch people (perhaps including the visionary him or herself)?
- How did their vision unite people?

Step Three: Once you feel complete with this particular visionary, repeat this process for at least two more people that come to mind when you think of visionaries.

Step Four: Go back and look at the answers you wrote in the "Attributes of their vision" column for each visionary and look for words or phrases that came up more than once. Circle these.

Step Five: Turn to a clean page in your journal and compile those repeated words and/or phrases from Step Four into one list called "Clues about my vision."

We will return to these in the Incorporation phase.

2. This activity will take 20-30 minutes a day over three days. It relates to the following passage in the chapter:

If the news stories that get our attention tend to be focused on what is missing in the world, it is our vision that provides the answer.

Step One: Sit down with a newspaper and your journal. Turn through the national and/or local section of the paper (skipping the sports and entertainment areas) and find an article that really seems to be calling to you, in other words, one that really gets your attention. You will know you have found the right one when you start to feel an emotional response when you read it. Once you have found this article, read it, and then move on to Step Two.

Step Two: Close your eyes and sit quietly thinking about the article you have just read. Allow the facts of the article (who, what, when, and where) to roll around in your head.

Now, take a deep breath and imagine there is a large funnel sitting between your head and your heart. The large open part of the funnel is about where your shoulders are and the small spout end leads into the area round your heart.

Imagine the facts of the story you have just read are pouring into the top of the funnel and only the essence of the story is getting through and coming into your heart.

Allow the essence of the story to rest in your heart space for a few moments before continuing.

Step Three: Open your eyes and begin writing about the story in your journal. Answer questions like the following:

- If the story was "good news," what was present in the situation being reported that made it so?
- If the story was "bad news," what was missing that, if present, might have changed the situation to "good news?"

Step Four: Repeat this activity over three separate days with three different articles. Choose a different article on a different subject each time you do this.

Step Five: After you have completed Step Four, look back over what you have written in your journal about each article and circle words or phrases that appear more than once.

Step Six: Turn to a clean page in your journal and compile those repeated words and/or phrases from Step Five into one list called "Clues about my vision."

We will return to these in the Incorporation phase.

3. If you enjoy free journaling, you might want to try this activity to gather clues about your vision. This activity can take as long or short a period of time as you would like to devote to it and could be done multiple times over several days for an even deeper experience.

Step One: Find a comfortable and quiet place to sit where you will not be disturbed for at least 30 minutes. Have your journal and a pencil or pen nearby. Close your eyes, take a few deep breaths, and let your body relax and your mind quiet. Now, ask this question:

"What kind of world do I want to live in?"

Spend a few moments simply sitting and pondering this question. Open your eyes and move on to Step Two.

Step Two: Open your journal to a blank page and start writing anything that comes up in response to the question, "What kind of world do I want to live in?"

Don't worry about making sense or writing complete sentences, just keep writing.

If the same word, phrase, or idea repeats itself, write it down each time it does so.

Don't stop your hand from moving, even if the words stop coming for awhile. If that happens, just keep making circles on the paper with your pencil or pen.

Stop the exercise only after the words have stopped flowing for the third time.

Step Three: Go back over what you have written and circle words or phrases that show up more than once.

Step Four: Turn to a clean page in your journal and compile those repeated words and/or phrases into one list called "Clues about my vision."

We will return to these in the Incorporation phase.

For additional resources, including free downloadable worksheets you might find helpful in completing these activities, please visit www.liveamythiclife.com.

Chapter 3

The Calling
Finding our purpose

The call comes and the hero has two choices: to follow it, or to refuse it. Whichever path is chosen, once the call has been heard, the hero's life will never be the same again.

> *The soul lives contented*
> *by listening,*
> *if it wants to change*
> *into the beauty of*
> *terrifying shapes*
> *it tries to speak.*
>
> -David Whyte

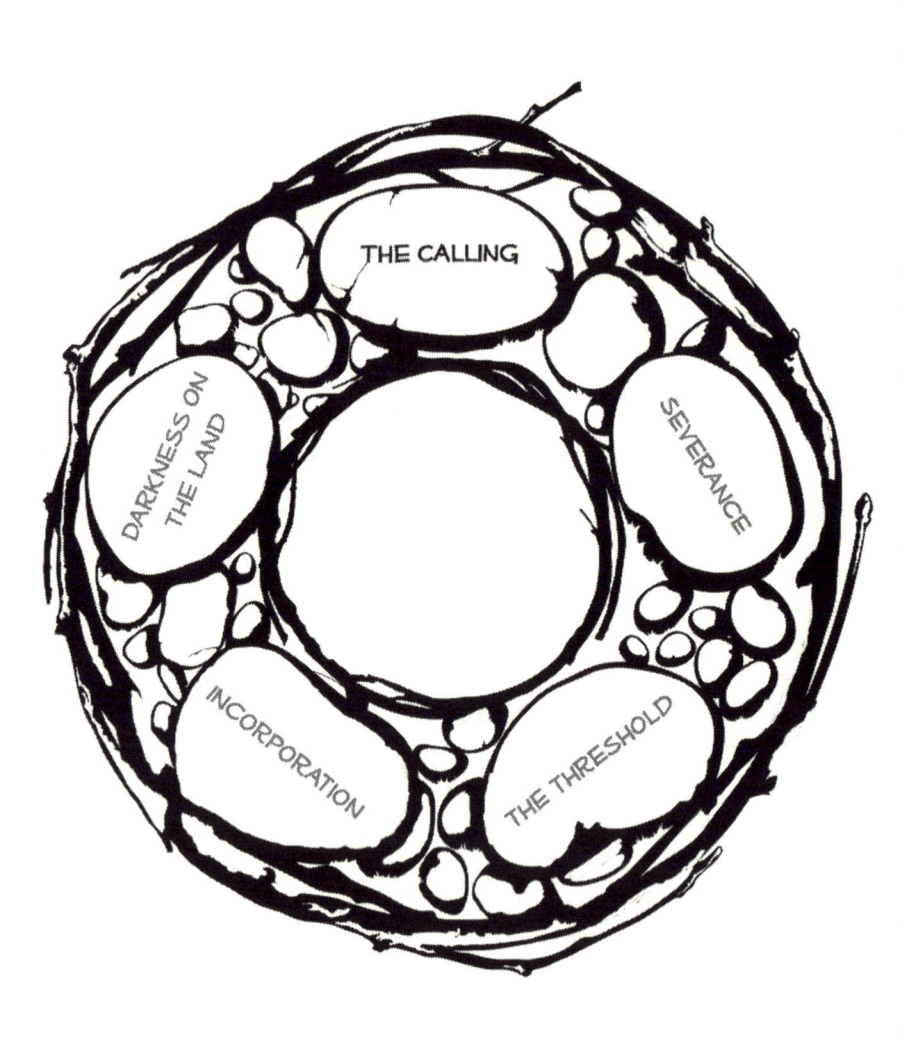

- THE CALLING
- SEVERANCE
- THE THRESHOLD
- INCORPORATION
- DARKNESS ON THE LAND

Chapter 3

Letter from Home: Listen to your heart above all other voices (Maria Kagen)—and then do what it says!

Peacemaker

Three days before the morning I awoke to the sound of the beating drum, I was driving through the Sierra Mountains in eastern California when I decided to stop for a cup of coffee. I was on my way to Big Pine in the Owens Valley where I would meet the guides and the rest of the group to begin my vision quest. I pulled into a little mountain town, parked the rental car along the main street, and walked a couple of blocks until I found a coffee shop. I was walking back to my car when I noticed I had parked in front of a gift shop, and I decided to walk inside.

As I looked around, the first things I saw were the typical souvenir t-shirts and postcards. I eventually noticed they also carried some nice-looking handcrafted Indian clay pots, blankets, and jewelry. Native American flute music played over the sound system, and the store had a warm, welcoming energy. I began to feel I had come into the store for a reason, but had no idea what it was.

Your Place in the World

I walked deeper into the store, looked up, and saw a peace pipe. It was hanging by itself on the back wall of the shop. Old feathers dangled from it with beads and a medicine bag, and it looked ancient and well used. The pipe captured my attention so completely, the rest of the shop seemed to fade into the background. For the longest time, I simply stood starring at it. In that moment, there was nothing in the world but the pipe and me. I knew I had to hold it.

I regained my senses and asked the woman working in the shop to take the pipe down for me. She got a stepladder, climbed up to retrieve it, and walked over to me carrying the pipe gently in front of her as if she were carrying an offering or sacred relic. I reached out and took it in both hands.

As I stood holding the pipe, I felt like I was holding something I had lost long ago. In finding it, I was once again whole and complete. I looked down at the pipe through blurry eyes. I shut them to keep from crying in front of a stranger, and when I did, I saw the face of an old Native American man. He had long gray hair and was wearing a robe, deep red in color and loosely wrapped around his shoulders. I felt my hands shaking and tried to steady them. In my mind, I backed away from what felt like a steep slope opening into the floor beneath my feet. Something inside told me to simply let go and allow this experience to take me wherever it might lead while another internal voice warned me to turn around before it was too late.

As I stood there in the shop with my eyes closed, I began to understand the old man I was seeing was a medicine man. His eyes told me he knew me very well, better even than I knew myself. He seemed to look right through the pin-striped mortgage banker to the seventeen-year-old boy standing on the jetty in Florida. I wondered if I was receiving the message I had come

Chapter 3: The Calling

to find, but things weren't unfolding the way I had expected them to on my quest, and I was feeling afraid of what this man in my mind might want to tell me. I began to pull away.

Just as the medicine man was about to speak, I opened my eyes and remembered where I was. The woman was nearby, watching me, and I felt embarrassed about the tears in my eyes and the length of time I had been standing there holding the pipe. "I need to think about this," I told the woman, and handed back the relic. As I did, she looked at me with knowing eyes, smiled, and said,

If it haunts you, you will know that it's yours.

I thanked her for her time, left the shop and drove out of town. As I did so, I thought about her words. There was no doubt in my mind something very big, much bigger than the pipe itself, *was* haunting me. I had ignored it for years as it whispered just below the level of my conscious awareness. It got my attention on the day my boss shared his good news with me. Whatever was haunting me inspired me to take the trip I was on. That morning, it grabbed me by the heart as I stood there in the gift shop fighting back tears.

I wondered about the pipe. What did it mean? Was the way I reacted to it the result of feeling particularly emotional that morning because of the vision quest I was ready to begin? Or was there some deeper message waiting for me in the coming days that was somehow connected to the pipe? One thing I knew for sure: I would have ample opportunities to think about the moment during the week ahead.

I had been back on the road for about thirty minutes when something happened. As if someone sitting in the passenger seat beside me spoke out loud, I heard the word "Peacemaker." At that very moment, I looked up through the windshield and saw a golden eagle directly over the road ahead of me. For some, the eagle is the bringer of vision. Knowing this, I pulled over and jumped out of the car to look for the eagle again, but it was gone. I stood there and shouted at the mountains around me, "Am I Peacemaker?" I wondered if I had just received another clue about the vision I had come to find.

After a few minutes, I collected myself enough to get back in the car and continue the drive. Less than five minutes later the largest coyote I have ever seen crossed the road no more than fifty yards ahead of me. There are those who believe the coyote is a great teacher who imparts wisdom by playing tricks. They might have counseled me to listen to the guidance I was receiving about being Peacemaker—but not to take it too literally! Looking back, I think it would have been good advice.

Needs, Wants and Yearnings

The chances are good that right now there is something you desire. Desires come in three forms: needs, wants, and yearnings. These kinds of desires correspond to the three kinds of lives we aspire to that I mentioned in the introduction: the pleasant life, the good life, and the mythic life.

First, we have **needs**. Needs are those material items required for us to live a pleasant life, like food, shelter, medical care, and education. Without first satisfying our needs, it is very difficult for us to go much further on our journey. If you are currently in an abusive relationship, your first need is to be safe. If you are not sure where the money is coming from for next month's rent because you just lost your job, then you need

Chapter 3: The Calling

to find work or some other means to pay your bills. We have to meet our needs first.

Once our needs are met, we become aware of another kind of desire: **wants**. Living the good life is primarily about satisfying our wants. We want certain material luxuries. We want work that is financially rewarding and emotionally satisfying. We want loving relationships and a vibrant and healthy body. We want our children to have opportunities for their own growth and development and to live their own version of the good life.

I grew up in what I would consider to be a fairly typical middle-class American family. My father worked for the power company and my mother worked part-time for the school system. Money was never plentiful in my family, and I can remember there was often a bit of a struggle to make the ends meet every month. Even so, we always seemed to have all we needed, and at least some of what we wanted.

My parents did an exceptional job of teaching me how to go about satisfying my needs and wants as I grew older. I was taught from an early age that I could achieve anything I could dream of doing; I could have anything I wanted, if I was willing to work hard enough. But I can't remember my parents speaking much about the third kind of desire we experience in life. If they did, it was probably in hushed tones that implied there was some danger associated with it. This third kind of desire is **yearning**, and it comes from the soul.

Yearning is sometimes experienced like an annoying neighborhood dog that barks all night and keeps us from getting a good night's sleep. The yearning nags at us, distracts us from our daily routines, and interferes with our ability to interact with the people around us the way we want to. It's always present, even

Your Place in the World

while we are focused on satisfying our needs and wants, but its voice tends to be drowned out by the noise of those other desires. Once we reach a point in life where our needs are met, and at least some of our wants are satisfied, we begin to wonder what else there is to life. This is the opening our yearning requires to finally be heard. This is when the haunting begins.

Yearning is a powerful force. Misunderstand it or misuse it and we can suddenly find our lives in shambles. Many of us make the mistake of thinking the yearning is originating somewhere outside ourselves. We mistakenly believe we will satisfy our yearnings by finding the right life partner, getting the promotion at work, or buying a bigger house. Sometimes we will go to any lengths to satisfy our yearnings by feeding it with material goods. In the process, we can end up losing touch with the things that are truly most important in life. But if we understand it properly, the power of yearning can lead us to a life of joy and meaning. Properly interpreted, our yearning leads us on a hero's journey into the mythic life.

The yearning will begin to work its power in us when we first begin to notice it's there. We may have denied it for a long time. We may need to release the feelings of guilt that often accompany this pull. If our lives are good, the fact we are not feeling completely satisfied might be confusing. After all, don't we have all we need and most of what we want? Haven't we been successful in the world? We may view the yearning as a sign we just can't be satisfied and see it as evidence of a personal shortcoming.

Or perhaps we have come to believe we will never have the life we desire. We feel we have failed so many times that success is not attainable. For some, the feeling of yearning is painful—just another way for the universe to tease us and set us up for failure. Looking into the face of our longing might bring memories of other losses and perceived failures, so we have learned not to do so at all.

There is great power in simply saying yes to our yearning, even if we are saying yes only to a small part of a bigger plan or idea. Saying yes starts a new vibration of energy within us and, eventually, in the space around us. Saying yes starts an attraction process that brings the things, people, and opportunities to us that will support us on our journey. When we say yes, we help to open the door to the other kind of life inside of us yearning to be lived.

> *Reflection question: Make a list of the things you need in your life and a separate list of the things you want in your life. Now, sit quietly for a while and answer this question: What do I yearn for? Do some journaling around the answer you get from asking this question and then compare it to the things you put on your lists of needs and wants. Do you see any connection between your yearnings and the clues you found about your vision in the previous chapter?*

The Call to Adventure and the Refusal

There are moments when the veil between the physical world of our daily lives and the world of imagination and possibility is thin. These experiences provide opportunities to glimpse into a way of being that, if we look deeply enough, just might change our lives. These moments can show up without warning. They can shake us and make us question all of our deeply held assumptions about who we are and our place in the world. These moments can be frightening and terrible, they can be filled with ecstatic joy and bliss, or they can be all of these things simultaneously. When yours occurs for you, do not forget you have invited it to happen by first saying *yes*.

In those moments when the veil is thin, the hero will experience what Joseph Campbell describes as "the call to adventure."[1] In mythological stories, a stranger knocks at the door, a child loses a ball that rolls under a bush, a path beckons in the woods, or some other event occurs interrupting the otherwise ordinary daily life of the hero. When the calling comes, the hero's life is never the same again. No matter how the hero responds, everything has changed. The story has begun, and once begun, it cannot be stopped.

In the myths, the call to adventure generally comes from somewhere outside the hero, and ours may as well, but even when outward events are calling us forth, they reflect a yearning from deep within. The pipe I held in the gift shop had no particular power in and of itself; it was simply serving as a mirror for something I already possessed. The next person to touch it probably had no reaction to it at all. Likewise, the eagle and the coyote might have been nothing more than interesting encounters with wild animals to another whose path they crossed. I was following my yearning, saying yes to begin my journey, and therefore ready and open to whatever mirror came my way.

Callings can take many forms. They can come gently, bringing a sense of peace and tranquility, and a moment of clarity about our lives and the way we are meant to live them. They can come powerfully, shaking us to our foundations and leaving us feeling lost, confused, or broken. A calling might show up

Chapter 3: The Calling

as a vague feeling of uneasiness. It might come as a desire to move to another town, change a job or career, or maybe change partners. It might show up as an illness or the loss of a loved one. Perhaps it's just a feeling something is breaking away or dissolving.

The call might be obvious, or it might be subtle, but it will almost always catch us by surprise. If we expect our calling to come in the form of a great spiritual awakening, it will happen in the moment we engage in a conversation with the letter carrier or hold some souvenir in a gift shop. The key is to stay awake and alert and have an open heart and mind.

In myths, the call comes and the hero has two choices: he or she can either answer it or not. There are times when the hero misses the clues or, worse yet, hears the call but chooses to ignore it. Campbell refers to this as the "refusal of the call,"[2] the consequences of which are never pleasant. In the myths, the refusal will result in visitations from spirits, deep sleep, the death of sons or daughters, or kingdoms turning to stone. Sometimes, the refusal results in the hero having to take an even more arduous path to fix what has been broken through his or her refusal.

When the hero refuses the call, he or she is essentially trying to lock down a current state of life, refusing to participate in the great cycle of birth and death, change and stasis. When we refuse the call, we are, in fact, making our own will into a god. When we do that, the call, or the perceived source of the call, becomes the enemy. The call becomes something to beat down, run from, or hide away. The call becomes a threat to the status quo, the accepted way of being, and is, therefore, to be avoided at all cost.

Your Place in the World

I have seen the effects of the refusal in myself and in others. Some can go most of their lives without being troubled by it much, at least outwardly. Then, the symptoms begin to show up in their later years. They begin to wonder about the choices they made. Where they the right ones? How might their lives have been different if they had taken the other road offered to them?

While the refusal might not be the path that shows up the most in the stories, I believe it is the most common response to the call in everyday life. Callings rarely ask us to do something that sounds sensible, and we can always find something else to do rather than spend the time and energy it would take to answer a calling. The thing to know is, in spite of any outward appearances, we always have a choice. We always have the power to choose for ourselves. We can ignore the call, hoping it will eventually go away, or we can listen and begin to look for its possible source.

I believe the refusal of the call is one of our greatest sources of pain. What would the world look like if each person "followed their bliss," as Campbell would advise? What if we all answered the hero's calling to serve only the highest good in ourselves and in others?

When I stood and held the peace pipe in the gift shop, I was being invited to claim something that had always been mine, yet I didn't feel worthy. I have come to understand callings are like that. They reflect back to us the true greatness that lies within us, a greatness we may rarely see and even find hard to believe exists. True callings will never come with a perfect road map attached, nor will they simply reconfirm something we already know about ourselves. Like visions, they will stretch us, perhaps nearly to our breaking point,

Chapter 3: The Calling

but in so doing, they pull out of us the beauty the world is waiting to see.

You may be thinking as you read this that callings are for other people, not you. You think you have never experienced a calling and don't expect to. I would ask you: Have you never yearned? Have you never sat and stared out a window and wondered what your life might look like if you had taken a different road, made another choice? Have you never regretted, even for a brief instant, following someone else's advice rather than setting out to discover on your own who you truly were? If any of this sounds familiar, then perhaps the only thing missing is one small "yes" from you.

> *Reflection question: Reflect on a time in your life you experienced a calling or some other form of very strong intuition or guidance about something you were to do or be. Did you follow the call? If so, where did it lead you? If not, why not? What were the outcomes from your decision? Spend some time writing about this in your journal.*

The Soul and our Purpose for Being

So, from where does this yearning emanate? From what source does the calling emerge, and what clue does it have to offer us about our hero's boon?

We are born with a particular, unique gift to share with the world—the purpose of our life. The yearning we feel, the call we experience, is the result of our purpose bumping up against the false ideas and beliefs we hold about ourselves. These ideas have brought us to where we are today, but they just aren't big

Your Place in the World

enough to contain our gift anymore. While our purpose might be hard to discern, it's there, nonetheless, and the yearning we feel and the calling we experience are signs it is time for us to bring our purpose into the world.

Purpose is the second part of the hero's boon. It serves to ground and bring form to our vision. While vision inspires us to dream about what *can* be done, purpose directs us to what is *ours* to do. When our vision and purpose are working together, it is a dance of equal partners, each informing the other, trading leads, and creating an inspired life and a beautiful world.

While we can express our purpose through our work or other roles we have in life, our purpose is not the job or role itself. Our purpose can be difficult to name; it is more like an energy, an attribute, or a passion. In a perfect scenario, we would all discover our gifts and also our own unique way to bring them into the world. But even then, it's not about the manner in which we bring our gifts into the world; it's about the gifts themselves.

A great feeling of freedom comes in understanding our purpose does not depend on filling particular roles. Once we understand this, we handle better the pain that sometimes accompanies the loss of a job or, for that matter, any other role we fill. As long as we define who we by a role in life, a relationship to another person, or any outward set of circumstances, we will feel lost when that outer circumstance changes. If we instead understand who we truly are is eternal and contained within us, we can feel whole and complete, no matter what external circumstances we face. Our purpose is eternal; the manner with which we bring purpose into the world is not and will change over time.

Let me offer a personal example. My purpose in life is to awaken and inspire a sense of vision and purpose in those who would lead an evolving world. One way I express my purpose is by leading wilderness vision quests. When I do that work, every part of my mind, heart, body, and soul are fully present and engaged, and there is nowhere else I would rather be or anything else I would rather be doing. What if I came to see my purpose in the world as being a vision quest guide but then could not physically do that work? If I saw my purpose as being a vision quest guide, I could end up being devastated. On the other hand, if I really understood my purpose was to awaken and inspire a sense of vision and purpose in those who would lead an evolving world, I might be disappointed I could no longer lead vision quests, but I would certainly be able to find other means to deliver my purpose.

As we set out to discover our purpose, we will look behind the form itself to the energy that supports it. Do not be concerned if the messages you begin to receive are ephemeral and illusive. Bringing form to our purpose is the work of the incorporation period.

Finding our Purpose

If we wish to find the second part of the hero's boon, purpose, then we need to journey into the land of the soul where it resides. If we journey into what might at first seem a strange and foreign place, then we need to understand the local language; the language of the soul.

The language of soul is a kind of communion rather than communication. The soul invites us into a deep connection rather than simple conversation. It doesn't use the lecture form of teaching, but rather, draws us in by offering far more questions than it ever answers. While we might ask our soul,

Your Place in the World

"Do I take the job offer from the bank or the insurance company," soul tells us, "You are Wind Walker," and in the process, invites us into a deeper journey of self-discovery, requiring further moments of communion.

Soul craves experience. Soul will push us to break down barriers, tear up our existing ideas about how our lives should look, and perhaps even give away all of our worldly possessions, just to experience the feelings those actions bring. Soul needs experience to grow and express itself in the world, and it doesn't care very much about outward appearances.

It also does not communicate in direct words but instead uses metaphor and symbolism to get our attention. It guides through feeling and intuition. Soul speaks to us in those moments we feel moved by a piece of music, a work or art, or a poem. We hear our souls speaking when we listen to the sounds of nature or, as strange as it may sound, carry on a conversation with a tree. As you look for your purpose, do not take your soul literally or be too quick to name the messages you are receiving. Instead, look for the meaning behind the metaphor.

There are three recurring themes in mythic stories that give us clues about how we can find our purpose. The first theme is "the hidden identity." In this story, a child of noble birth is hidden among common people to protect the child from a menace of some kind. The child grows up with a vague sense they don't belong with the family that raised them but are not sure just where or to whom they do belong. Throughout their lives, they get clues about their origin but can never quite find the answer they seek. Finally, something happens that calls them to begin a

Chapter 3: The Calling

process of discovery, and they come to understand not only who they are and where they have come from but also the destiny they were born to fulfill.

We are all of noble birth, and each of us has come into the world with a particular place of belonging and a people to serve. If we follow our own story backward to our childhood and spend time reflecting, we would likely remember a particular moment when we were doing something that felt absolutely wonderful, like it was something we were born to do, and no one else could do this thing in the unique way we could. It might have been something as simple as building sand castles on the beach, walking the family dog, or acting in the school play. Everyone has had one of those moments when time seemed to stand still. I call these "soul moments" because they are the times when the veil between our everyday life and our soul is thinnest and we are most directly in a place of soul-communion.

Once we have remembered a soul moment, we can find other places in our life where we have had similar experiences. These moments supported the message of our soul, reinforcing the earlier experience in a vital way. It is easy, as we go about our daily lives, to lose touch with our early soul moments. Most of us don't have much experience listening to our souls and the daily world of clocks, financial responsibilities, and family commitments often don't promote soul development, but soul keeps giving us clues along the way. We find these clues in the activities we do that bring us deep joy and put us in a state of bliss.

When the hero has heard the call and begun his journey, a second theme emerges in the myths that I refer to as "challenges along the way." Heroes encounter a variety of monsters, temptations, and other difficulties as they search for their boon.

Your Place in the World

(Odysseus' story, which I mentioned in Chapter 1, is one example of this.) Each time the hero encounters one of these challenges, another part of their true identity is revealed, or they find some clue about what to do next to get closer to their goal.

We experience our own kind of challenges and difficulties in life, as well. Each time we encounter our own form of monster, we have another opportunity to discover something essential about ourselves. While we grow and learn much in the quiet, peaceful moments of our lives, it is in difficult times that we have the opportunity to understand ourselves on a deeper level. Sometimes our deepest wounds reveal our most precious and sacred gifts. While they might be difficult and painful to look at, our wounds give us powerful clues about the person we were born to be.

We have all heard stories about people who survive cancer, assault, divorce, or any number of other difficult and challenging life circumstances to come away from the experience with new-found understanding about their purpose. Perhaps you are one of these people yourself. Sometimes a new purpose in life is found through an activity, such as when a cancer survivor councils others facing the disease. But often, the gift found in the wound is a deeper and richer understanding of the preciousness of life itself, about the strength that comes from facing our greatest fears and living through them.

The third theme in mythic stories that will instruct us in how to find our purpose is that of the "wise elder." Often, someone will show up at just the moment when the hero needs assistance. It might be a wizard, a fairy godmother, or a magical creature. These helpers bring with them knowledge and experience the hero will need on his journey, and they often play a crucial role in the discovery of the hero's boon.

Chapter 3: The Calling

We have all had "wise elders" in our lives, even when we failed to notice their arrival. While the path ahead is ours to walk, we don't have to travel it alone. This path, or one very much like it, has been walked before, and we will do well to ask for and accept help from others along the way. Our own version of a wise elder might take the form of a councilor or therapist, a minister or priest, or an uncle or aunt who has made their own journey to their soul. The wise elder is not always a person; it could be a book, movie, or song that gives us the message we need at just the time we need it.

No matter what form the wise elders take in myths, they always have one thing in common: while they offer guidance to the hero, they allow the hero to walk their own path and reach their own conclusions. As we seek out our helpers along the way, we should look for this important characteristic, as well. Their advice and guidance are valuable, but we must make our own journeys to our souls. No one else can do that for us.

The path into soul to find purpose can be circuitous. I sometimes wish the soul was easier to understand, but then I think about how rich my life is from wandering the path. Perhaps by cutting across some of the oxbows of the river of my life I might make quicker progress. Perhaps I could then get more done in the time I have been given. But whom would I have missed meeting and loving? What experiences would I have not been able to learn from? Though I sometimes look into the mirror and wish they would go away, the lines and scars on my face give it character and depth. The same is true for the gifts I offer the world.

Your Place in the World

> **Reflection question:** *Looking back, can you think of a time when your soul was trying to "speak" to you? Perhaps it was through a soul moment, a challenge in your life, or a wise elder? Describe the experience. How were the messages communicated? How did you interpret them? What were the outcomes?*

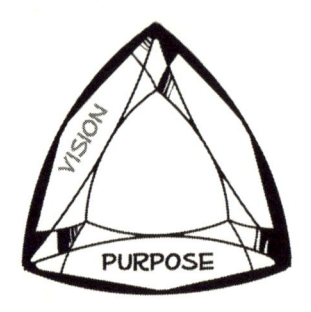

VISION

PURPOSE

We Can't Do Anything Else

Imagine for a moment you are a reporter visiting Albert Einstein late in his life. You are a great admirer of Einstein and have been trying to get an interview with him for years. Finally, you get your moment with the famous man and ask: "Dr. Einstein, you are one of the great thinkers, one of the greatest minds in all of human history. Your theories have helped the rest of us to see the universe differently. Your ideas span both science and spirituality. You have impacted our world now and for generations to come. But I am wondering, Dr. Einstein, just what do *you* think of your accomplishments? What do *you* think of the work you have done?" And the great man replies with a deep sigh, "Oh…It's a living."

Chapter 3: The Calling

Can you imagine that scenario? Can you imagine Einstein saying something like, "You know, if I could have done anything, I would have been an accountant! Ah, that would be my bliss." What about Gandhi saying: "You know, being a lawyer isn't so bad. I've been to University and got my degree and everything. Why would I want to give that up to travel the countryside barefoot in a robe?" Or this conversation between Jesus and God: "Okay, Pop. I hear what you're telling me about this preaching thing, but I kind of like the carpenter gig. I've been working at it a few years and building up my 401K. Why would I want to leave it now? I'll tell you what, let's talk again when I get closer to retirement. I should be able to fit this healing thing in then."

None of this is meant to disparage accountants, lawyers, or carpenters. Einstein, Gandhi, and Jesus are simply three examples of people who answered their callings, followed their passions, and changed the world in the process. What would our world look like today if they had said no to their callings?

I had a friend who once told me she became a minister because she had decided she couldn't do anything else. I laughed a bit thinking she was poking fun at her skill sets but then realized what she meant. She had come to a point in her life where her calling to the ministry was so strong she simply could not do anything *but* follow it.

The world isn't changed by people who ignore their callings. The world is changed by people who are fully immersed in living their passions, by people who wake up every day with a clear understanding of who they are and what they were born to do—and then are actually doing it. Sure, there will be times of doubt, times when you will feel weary and question why

Your Place in the World

you even bother, but you will push on—because you can't do anything else.

How will you know when you are not on your path? My experience is most of us know, even if we don't want to admit it. Our internal guidance systems let us know when we are living from our deepest truths and when we are off track. What stands between our guidance and our awareness are the artificial barriers we have constructed over the years. Our egos want to maintain control, and sometimes we let them, but deep inside we know why we are here and what we should be doing.

The reality for most of us is that discovering our purpose requires more that a one-time journey to soul. Most of us don't find our path, start our journey, and then never wander from it. Being true to our path requires constant monitoring. It means something else too: we must always stand ready to abandon it for a truer one. We must continually return to soul, asking, "What's next?"

The clue to knowing we are not on our path is the yearning we feel when we have drifted away. The longing deep inside for something else is the sign we need to look deeper. So embrace the sense of yearning you feel. Make friends with the ache in your chest, the knot in your stomach, or however it reveals itself for you. We should no more curse the yearning than we should the road that carries us home at the end of the day's work. The metaphor is appropriate; our yearning is the path that carries us home.

To be comfortable with our yearning, we must learn to be comfortable living in a state of mystery. We have to give up on our false sense of control and our need to know. We need to be prepared to live for awhile in a state of not-knowingness. To trust in yearning implies a faith in the unknown.

Chapter 3: The Calling

You will find the final and most powerful clue to your purpose when you arrive at the place in your life where *you can't do anything else*. Nothing else matters as much as delivering your purpose to the world. When you discover your purpose, the mystery of how to bring it into reality won't deter you; it will simply encourage you to *be* this one particular unique gift you were born to embody.

Imaginal Cells

The lowly caterpillar has something to teach us about the subject of callings. At a certain point in its life, the caterpillar begins to consume vast quantities of food. It can sometimes strip a plant bare of foliage in a day, thereby creating a serious problem for itself—it's out of food with no apparent solution at hand.

Fortunately for the caterpillar, it has within it something called imaginal cells. These cells contain the blueprint for the salvation of the caterpillar. At just this crossroads in the caterpillar's life, at a time when all of its options seem to be gone, the imaginal cells become activated and begin instructing the caterpillar in the art of building a cocoon. I can almost imagine the internal dialogue going on in the caterpillar's little brain: *You fool! You are wasting time creating this ugly thing when you should be looking for a new bush to eat*! But build on it does.

Once fully inside the cocoon, amazing things happen. First, the imaginal cells begin to multiply. The caterpillar's body interprets the cells to be foreign and a danger to the caterpillar, so it fights back, much like our own white blood cells fight off infection or the way we often tend to resist major changes in our lives. The imaginal cells are beaten back for a while, but eventually they multiply at a rate that simply takes over the caterpillar, and its body starts to dissolve into goo. The forces of stasis are no match for the forces of change, and the caterpillar is no more.

The next step is even more miraculous, for somehow the cells, only days before organized into a form known as caterpillar, rearrange themselves into the beautiful creature called butterfly. In spite of the dire circumstances, in spite of the struggle, the answer to the challenge facing the caterpillar comes forth from within its very being. Finally, the butterfly emerges from the cocoon.

In his book *Blessed Unrest*, Paul Hawken describes what he calls "the largest movement in the world."[3] It is a movement of movements, with people all over the planet coming together, not behind a single leader or specific cause, yet united by a commitment to create a world that works for everyone.

I see the people Hawken describes like human caterpillars being called to start spinning their cocoons by the power of their yearnings. They might not yet have any idea why they are doing the work, nor do they have a clear picture of the butterfly to come on the other side of this threshold; they only know they must do it—or die trying—*because they can't do anything else*. Some are deep in the goo-like stage of complete transformation and unsure where to go next. Others are playing the role of the imaginal cells. All are the heroes of our time.

There is one more aspect about callings to understand before we move forward. Callings are not the answers themselves; they are the sign it is time to start a journey. When I stood in the gift shop and wondered if the message I was getting was the answer I had been looking for, I was missing the point. The pipe wasn't a sign I was receiving my answer; it was a sign I was just starting my journey. That's what callings are for. They grab our attention in order to get us to start looking. While it might be tempting to stop here and build our identity around the calling itself, we would be missing the rest of a very important journey.

The Response

This chapter began with some lines of poetry from David Whyte:

> *The soul lives contented*
> *by listening,*
> *if it wants to change*
> *into the beauty of*
> *terrifying shapes*
> *it tries to speak.*

Our souls have been trying to speak to us all of our lives with mixed results. If soul is unable to get its point across, it will roar, or turn itself into one of Whyte's "terrifying shapes." Our dreams speak to us, even when we are awake. If we don't listen, they speak a little louder. Eventually, they *will* get our attention.

Our callings can bring up fear while they awaken us with the knowledge that once experienced, nothing will ever be the same. Like Pandora's Box, which once opened can never again be closed, our calling can never again be ignored. Campbell says in *The Hero with a Thousand Faces*:

> *But whether small or great, and no matter what the stage or grade of life, the calling rings up the curtain, always, on a mystery of transfiguration—a rite, or moment, of spiritual passage, which, when complete, amounts to a dying and a birth. The familiar life horizon has been outgrown; the old concepts, ideals, and emotional patterns no longer fit; the time for the passing of a threshold is at hand.[4]*

There is still some mystery left in this universe, not the least of which is the mystery of our souls. This mystery speaks to us through our callings, and we are beckoned to follow. We do so with the full understanding we are beginning a journey with no end. It is the journey of a life well lived.

Activities

The following are designed to help you uncover clues about your purpose. Do at least one before moving on to the next chapter.

At this stage, you are looking for clues, not final answers, so don't be concerned if what you find here doesn't make much sense to you. We will work with making sense of the clues in the Incorporation phase.

If you have difficulty doing these activities, try rereading the section in the chapter titled *Finding our Purpose*. You might also want to visit www.liveamythiclife.com where you will find worksheets you can download and use for these activities.

1. This activity relates to the idea of "hidden identity" from the chapter. This process will take 30-60 minutes, depending on how much time you want to devote to it. Find a comfortable place to sit where you will not be disturbed. Have your journal and a pencil or pen nearby.

    Step One: Close your eyes and take a few breaths. Allow your mind to wander back to a time in your childhood. See yourself at the age of 12 or younger. Take a moment just to visualize yourself at this age, allowing as much detail to appear as possible.

    Next, see if you can recall a moment in your childhood when you were engaged in an activity where you felt completely and totally "at home." Time may have seemed to stand still. You were immersed in the experience and whatever you were doing seemed to come almost effortlessly.

Once you have a memory like this, spend a few moments just observing the child-you in your mind doing this activity.

As you recall this memory, do you notice a physical sensation anywhere in your body? If you are unsure about this question, close your eyes again and bring the memory back. Be aware of any energy you might be feeling and notice where it is centered in your body.

Step Two: Now, take a few more deep breaths, and think about an activity you engage in now, as an adult. When you do this activity, time seems to stand still. You feel completely in your element and empowered. It doesn't matter to you if you are doing this activity the correct way, based on someone else's definition of correct, or are doing it well, based on someone else's definition of well, but you are simply doing it.

Allow this activity to come to your mind and sit with it for awhile just observing yourself doing it. Do you notice a similar physical sensation or energy in your body as you experienced during your childhood memory? This energy is a sign you have found a thread connecting the two memories and provides a powerful clue about your purpose.

Step Three: Turn to a clean page in your journal and write "Clues about my purpose" at the top of the page. Record your answers to the following questions on this page.

- What similarities do you see between what you found in Step One and Step Two? Is there a common theme, feeling, or emotion?

- Look for words or short phrases that describe the basic essence of the activities you have been thinking about during this activity.

2. This activity relates to the idea of "Challenges along the Way" from the chapter. This process will take 30-60 minutes, depending on how much time you want to devote to it. Find a comfortable place to sit where you will not be disturbed. Have your journal and a pencil or pen nearby.

Step One: Take a few deep breaths, close your eyes, and think about one particular challenge or difficulty you have experienced in your life. It is best to pick one you have already made it through as opposed to something you are dealing with right now. When you are ready, open your eyes. Reflect back on the challenge or difficulty and how you made your way through it, and make some notes in your journal about the following:

- Briefly describe the challenge or difficulty. What were you like at the beginning of this period? What are you like today? How have you changed?

- What were the inner resources or personal traits you discovered about yourself through the process of dealing with the challenge or difficulty?

Hint: Resist the temptation to settle on the first thing that comes to mind. Keep asking for more information. For example, if the answer that comes to you is something like, "I learned I was strong and could stand on my own two

Your Place in the World

feet," keep challenging this answer with questions like the following: How was I strong? How do I know I was strong? What evidence was there?

Step Two: Turn to a clean page in your journal and write "Clues about my purpose" at the top of the page. Look back over the notes you took in Step One of this activity for words, phrases, or ideas that come up repeatedly and that resonate with you. Record them on this page.

3. This activity relates to the idea of "Wise Elders" from the chapter. This process will take 30-60 minutes, depending on how much time you want to devote to it. Find a comfortable place to sit where you will not be disturbed. Have your journal and a pencil or pen nearby.

Step One: Think for a moment about those people, Wise Elders, who have been influential in your life. They might be people you know, characters in a book, or the visionaries you listed in the activity at the end of Chapter Two. Open your journal and make a list of all the Wise Elders who have come into your life. Pick the three you think have had the most influence on you and answer the following questions for each one:

- What are, or were, this Wise Elder's attributes, personal gifts, and/or mission in the world?
- If you knew them personally, what did they teach you about yourself? If you didn't know them personally, imagine you are having a conversation with

them. What advice do you think they would offer you about finding your purpose in life?

Step Two: Go back over your notes in Step One and circle the words or phrases that showed up more than once. Turn to a clean page in your journal and write "Clues about my purpose" at the top of the page. Record on this page the words or phrases you just circled.

For additional resources, including free downloadable worksheets you might find helpful in completing these activities, please visit www.liveamythiclife.com.

Chapter 4

Severance

Serving our people

Before the hero can step fully and completely into the threshold experience, he must let go of the world he has known and open his hands, mind, and heart to accept that which is meant to be.

> *It is easier for a rope to pass through the eye of a needle than for a rich man to enter into the kingdom of God.*
>
> *- Jesus the Christ*

> *Give up all the other worlds except the one to which you belong.*
>
> *- David Whyte*

> *When I let go of what I am, I become what I am meant to be.*
>
> *-Lao Tzu*

THE CALLING

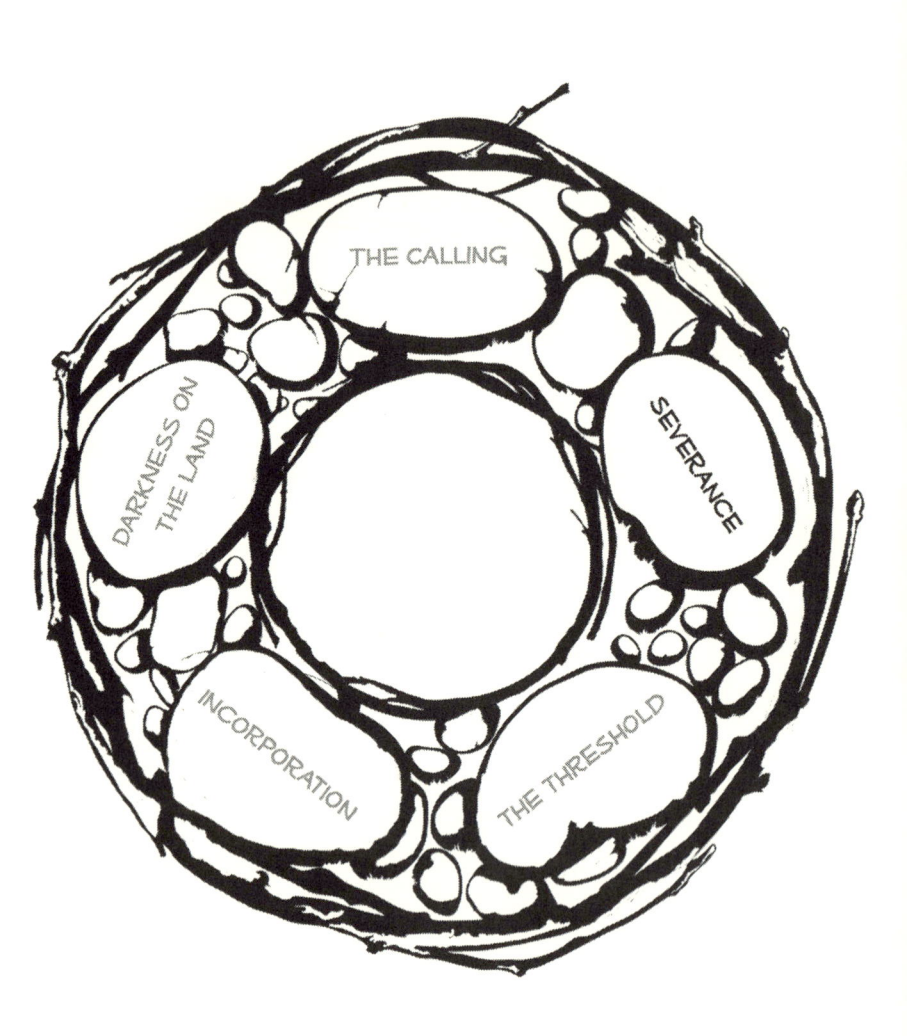

SEVERANCE

THE THRESHOLD

INCORPORATION

DARKNESS ON THE LAND

Chapter 4

Letter from Home: I'm so proud of you. This is such a big step, both inside and outside. I'm not so sure I would be up for this sort of challenge but I know you are. You are ready for this and whatever is revealed. Somehow I know your soul has been waiting for this very time. So, go easy on yourself. Relax, and don't forget to breath! I'll hold you close in my heart knowing Divine Order is unfolding in Its perfect way.

Everything

After my encounter with the pipe, the eagle, and the coyote, I continued driving south toward Big Pine. An hour later, I arrived at the campground where the rest of the group was waiting. We began our time together by sitting in council and sharing our stories: who we were, why we had come, and what we expected to receive from our quest.

Shortly after lunch we were invited to go for a solitary walk. I threw a few things, including a wooden flute, into a small pack and set off along a path next to a creek that ran through the campground. Eventually, the path turned away from the creek, heading up a hillside into an area of cactus and rocks. I had neglected to bring sunscreen, so I decided to look for a shady spot next to the creek. I found a wide, flat rock next to the water and protected from the sun by thick, overhanging branches, and sat down.

The creek was about ten feet wide, with water tumbling over large rocks just upstream and forming a small pool at my feet. The water was so clear I could see to the bottom, and as I looked into it, I noticed something was looking back at me. A beautiful trout slowly swam just below the surface, only a few feet away. It seemed to be watching me intently. As my eyes adjusted, I noticed the pool was home to several "keeper" trout; and I wished I had brought my fly rod along. But since I wasn't going to catch any of these fish, I decided to sit and watch them instead.

Although most of the trout were swimming around, doing their trout thing, the first one I noticed seemed perfectly contented to hang just below the surface, watching me. Having nothing else to do and nowhere else to go for a while, I started to talk to the trout. I introduced myself to him and told him why I was there. I shared a bit about my life, and then I apologized for my first thoughts of trying to impale his lip with a number 12 dry fly.

I don't remember exactly what I said to him, but I do recall he was a good listener, so good I wanted to do something to thank him for his time. I remembered the flute in my pack and took it out to play for him in gratitude. As I played, rocking back and forth in time to the music, my new friend floated there in the water, listening.

And then, as it had happened earlier that day in the car, I heard a voice ask, *What do you want?* I answered in my thoughts; *I want to know if I am Peacemaker.* I continued to play my flute, afraid if I stopped the magic of the moment would end. As the tears ran down my face, the next question that came to my mind was: *What are you willing to give?*

Chapter 4: Severance

There are moments in time that are turning points, dividing lines that, once crossed, change our lives. I didn't know it then, but that particular moment was just such a dividing line for me. There beside the stream, I made a deal with my soul. I did not stop to consider the consequences of my response. *Everything,* I said, and as if I had vanished from the face of the earth, I stepped fully and completely into the threshold, and nothing has been the same for me since.

The Ending that is a Beginning

As Joseph Campbell would tell us, every hero's journey begins with an ending and ends with a beginning. The severance is the ending that begins it all. The process of severance actually starts the very moment we begin to notice a calling. It might include a time of preparation, or it might happen suddenly. We complete the process when we finally let go of whatever we have been holding onto and begin our journey.

In a figurative sense, the severance calls us to leave our current idea of home in order to find our true home, our place in the world. In myth, the hero will often step through a doorway, dive into a pool of water, or take a new path through the woods. A more modern example of severance is found in *The Hobbit* by J. R. R. Tolkien. The hero of the story, Bilbo Baggins, is perfectly happy living close to the home of his birth, staying safe and snug in his tidy little burrow of a house in the side of a hill. One day everything changes for Bilbo when he is called by the wizard, Gandalf the Grey, to take a journey. Something in Bilbo tells him this is something he must do, but venturing from his homeland terrifies him. For Bilbo, simply leaving home is a victory. This one decision ends up changing Bilbo's life and the history of his world.

Accumulating Layers vs. Traveling Light

So many influences in our world tell us that more is better, that the secret to happiness is adding to, not taking away. We find it difficult to understand we must subtract some things from our lives in order to find the source of our calling. Before we can begin our journey, we must let go of where we are.

The journey into the threshold, which can only begin after the severance, is one the hero can better make if he is traveling light. When we are called to find the source of our yearning, we are simultaneously called to release those things that no longer serve us.

Here is an image to illustrate this idea. Imagine there is a flashlight on the table in front of you. It is turned on and shining brightly, representing you at the moment of your birth. Contained in this light is all the information you need to understand your vision, your purpose, and the way you are to serve in the world. If someone could read this light, they would be able to tell exactly why you were born. Now, imagine there is a small sheet of colored tissue paper placed over the light. This sheet might represent the first time you felt shame in your life. Another sheet of colored paper is placed over the light, perhaps representing the time a well-meaning adult said you were smart and should grow up to make a lot of money. Now, another sheet of paper appears, representing the first job you took to pay the bills, in spite of your total lack of interest in the field. Now, another sheet is placed over the others, this one representing a major set-back or a time of deep personal pain. In spite of all

Chapter 4: Severance

the sheets of paper, some light is still getting through, but it's harder to see. One after another, the layers of your life continue to accumulate until, finally, the light you were born with can no longer be seen.

Then one day something happens. You experience a calling, and it's as though someone took a sharp object and suddenly poked a hole through all those layers of paper. You catch a glimpse, if only for a moment, of the radiance hidden beneath, and, although it might be a little scary, you like what you see. You decide to look a little further to find out what you can about the source of the light. Only, what will you do about all those sheets of paper? Some of them are pretty important; others you have built your identity around. Those sheets have helped you to feel safe in the world, and perhaps even brought you wealth and recognition. Is there room in the pack you plan to carry on this journey for all of those sheets?

A month before I was to leave for my vision quest, I began to gather the equipment I would need for the trip. I purchased a backpack in which to carry six days' worth of clothing, gear, and food. In the weeks before leaving, I stared laying everything I thought I would need on the floor of my basement, sorting the "have-to-haves," from the "like-to-haves." I got a good laugh the first time I tried to stuff everything into my backpack and discovered there wasn't nearly enough room for it all—plus, I couldn't lift it!

In the process of planning my packing, I started to see how all that stuff on the floor was a metaphor for parts of my life. Although packing the camping gear was a short term necessity, it revealed my need to sort the essential from the nonessential in my life in general. How much of what I was carrying around was important? How much was unnecessary? And where did

Your Place in the World

all that stuff come from, anyway? I began to ask two questions about my life: What was I willing to give up, and what was nonnegotiable? I took a personal inventory; I began to separate the things that were not essential from those that really mattered. I wanted to know what could go and where I drew my line in the sand. The answers came fairly quickly. In spite of all the good things I had in my life, I was willing to let them all go except for my wife and my children. Everything else was on the table.

The severance process is like packing for a trip, only this trip might be for the rest of your life. It's an opportunity to separate all those sheets of paper, look at them one by one, and decide what stays with you for the threshold ahead, and what is released. Those sheets of paper might be personal belongings, relationships, responsibilities, or any number of other things. Only you know what's weighing you down and what's essential to keep.

How will you know what stays and what goes? There are some activities at the end of this chapter to help you with this process, but for now, continue to use the metaphor of packing for a trip. Begin to make choices based on the image you have of the road of life ahead rather than the one you have left behind, and then think about what you want to carry with you. If something seems important to keep, ask yourself where it came from. Did you intentionally choose it, or did someone else give it to you, whether you asked for it or not? If you intentionally chose it, would you choose it again given another chance?

My severance process started in the months leading up to my vision quest and concluded beside the creek when I answered, *Everything,* fully opening the door for the threshold experience that followed. Will you need to release everything? I don't have

Chapter 4: Severance

an answer for that. I believe it depends on where you are on your journey. In my case, I had come to a point where it felt as if my life simply could not go on working as it had. Would I have gotten some answers on my vision quest without the experience by the creek? Yes, probably so. Would those answers have been the same, and would they have led me to the same place I am in today? Part of me thinks not, but in truth, who knows?

This I do believe to be true: Whatever has gotten us to where we are will not carry us into the life of our dreams. If we have had success in life based on one set of assumptions about the way the world works, it will be necessary to let them go to create what seems impossible in our lives. If something seems impossible, it's because we don't yet know how to make it happen. If we did, we would already have done so. To make the seemingly impossible come true, we have to let go of the way we have been operating, even those ways that have brought us success, before we can move on. This is the essence of the severance.

As we make choices between what we should release and what we should keep, we become simpler, lighter, and more focused. As we become lighter, it becomes easier to see our truth the closer we get to it. It is paradoxical but true, the more we can release the richer we become. The richer we become, the more we can release.

When I was a kid, my younger brother and I had an annual ritual during the first few days of Christmas break. My mother made us spend half a day cleaning out our closets. If we hadn't played with a toy for the past year, it had to be donated. Other kids who didn't have as much as we did could use the toy, we were told. We were willing to go through this process because our mother promised us by doing so we were making room for all the new things Santa would bring us in just a few days. I didn't know it at the time, but I was learning an important metaphysical lesson: when we clear out space in our lives by releasing what no longer serves us, we create a vacuum the universe will quickly rush to fill. We have the power to decide how we want to fill the space, but the space must first be created.

In his influential book *Good to Great*, business consultant Jim Collins writes about principles various business leaders have employed to help their enterprises make quantum jumps in profitability. He uses the metaphor of a bus to a represent a business. In order to move a business in the right direction, a leader needs to get the right people on the bus and get the wrong people off. The message is that one way to make a quantum leap with your business is to recruit people, not simply for skill sets, but for attitude and commitment to an ideal. By getting the right people on the bus and moving the wrong people off, a business leader can get the bus moving in the right direction at top speed.[1]

What if we were to look at the idea from the perspective of the people on the bus rather than the bus driver? How do you know you are on the right bus? What if, somewhere along the line, you accidentally stepped onto the wrong bus, headed in the wrong direction, and then, to top it all off, you grabbed the first seat you saw and now find you are in the wrong seat, as well? Do you stay committed to the bus? Do you just give up and let the bus decide your destination and how you get there? Or do you take the next opportunity to get off the bus, look around a little, and then, deliberately this time, choose another bus?

The bus could be a metaphor for a job, a relationship, or any other situation. Some of us have been on the bus for so long, we have become accustomed to the seat—it fits our butts if not our souls. We are driving through some scary-looking neighborhoods, and our bus feels comfortable and safe. All the while, we keep getting the feeling we are not where we are supposed to be. We don't seem to have much in common with the other people around us. Some of them are passionately committed to the ride; others appear to be as unsure as we are. Still, since it's the bus we stepped onto so long ago, it must me the right one. Right?

Stepping off the bus you have been riding can be the most difficult thing you ever do. The very idea of doing so can bring up fear and resistance. In stepping off the bus, a kind of death occurs. It is the death of your old life, your old way of being, and you might have to make the decision to leave your seat before the next bus has made its appearance. Getting off the bus requires faith there will be another one coming along. It requires a willingness to take chances, to trust the universe to support you. It requires commitment, as well, a commitment to your soul. You must be committed to living from your soul to a greater degree than you are committed to your current level of comfort and security. Being on the right bus can make all the difference in your life and the lives of those meant to ride along with you.

You have the power to be who you want to be. This is not a call to take on yet another burden; rather, it is a suggestion it might be time to release a few. Choose again. It's okay to do so; in fact, it's required. To live a life truly free and unlimited, we have to constantly make choices about what to keep and what to release. If the old pair of pants doesn't fit anymore, it might be time to release them to the thrift store. If the old idea or role just doesn't seem fit anymore, then let it go.

As you step into the process of severance, you may feel some grief. Jesus said, "Blessed are they who mourn, for they shall be comforted."[2] I don't know why, but there seems to be something about the human heart that it needs to be cracked open in order to expand and grow. In moments of loss, whether those losses are the big, life-changing kind or the small every day adjustments, opportunities are created for new discoveries, for gifts of great value to be revealed. The severance is a kind of cracking open. Have faith, the light will come; in fact, it's already there within you just waiting to shine out.

> *Reflection question: Pause at this point and think about one particular aspect of your life. Maybe it's your job, a personal relationship, or an activity you engage in. It might also be a particular idea or attitude about life. Go with whatever comes to your mind first. Reflect on how you picked up the paper, added the thing to your suitcase, or got on the bus—to borrow metaphors from the previous section. How does it look and feel to you now? What do you think it might it feel like to let it go? Do this for as many different parts of your life as you can think of. Then make some notes about this experience in your journal.*

Chapter 4: Severance

A Guard at the Gate

So far on your journey, you have received clues about your vision in the voice of Spirit, and you have begun to understand your purpose in the language of the soul. As you stand at the edge of the threshold and contemplate the possibility of a process of severance, it is very likely another sound will begin to get your attention: the cry of the ego.

I introduced the idea of ego in Chapter 1, but now it is time to take a deeper look at this part of ourselves. At this stage of the journey the ego will try everything possible to get us to stop and turn back for the safety of known waters before we get in too deep. After all, the ego only knows what we have told it through our interpretations of our life experiences and the cultural influences we have accepted. Its primary job is to remind us about how good all the accumulated parts of our current life are. If we try something new, like shedding old ideas about who we are so our true nature can be revealed, the ego is going to warn us about all the reasons why we would never want to do that. The ego assumes if we picked up the sheet of colored paper, packed it in our suitcase, and got on the bus with it, then we really want and need it. In fact, our egos have been active all our lives helping us with our wants and needs, but now that we are dealing with yearnings, the ego will need retraining.

There is an image you might find useful as you contemplate dealing with a complaining ego: the Loyal Soldier.[3] This is a metaphor that derives from incidents following World War II. Allied forces found Japanese soldiers who had been left behind to defend positions on islands in the South Pacific. When these men were discovered, they had no idea the war was over and often refused to believe it had ended, in spite of evidence to the contrary. They had been trained to fight to the death in the defense of a cause, and their minds could not conceive the cause had been lost.

The Loyal Soldier represents an aspect of our ego that arose in us at an early age. It was the Loyal Soldier's responsibility to protect us from physical, emotional, and psychological harm. We hear his or her voice when we start to step beyond our normal boundaries and experience the world in a new way. We hear the Loyal Soldier's voice when we start to extend ourselves in a way that could, quite possibly, result in embarrassment or failure. Early in our lives, our Loyal Soldiers were given orders to protect us as all costs, and they continue to do so today.

When we were young and growing, the Loyal Soldier had an important role to play. The Loyal Soldier warned us when we began to do something physically dangerous. Before we were mature enough to handle the pain, it warned us when we began to do something that might harm us emotionally. Like a protective nanny, the Loyal Soldier watched over us as we grew into adults. The problem is, the Loyal Soldier has never been given new orders. Like the Japanese soldiers who never received word the war was over, our Loyal Soldier is still fighting the battles of childhood, warning us about risks and keeping us safe.

What shall we do with this character? The first thing to know it is useless trying to convince the Loyal Soldier the war is over. The Loyal Soldier is too dedicated to the cause to listen to anything that would contradict it. Instead, we can take some guidance from the manner in which the Japanese people dealt with their soldiers after the war. First, they welcomed their soldiers home and honored them as the heroes they were. Second, they thanked them profusely for the valiant way in which they had served their country. Next, they gently and repeatedly reminded them the war was over. Finally, once the soldiers had begun to reintegrate into society, they were assigned new tasks and given causes appropriate for the time and circumstances.

A fully mature and appropriately directed Loyal Soldier can actually be an asset in the incorporation phase, but one who is still focused on protecting a child can be a huge block to severance and threshold experiences. If we can learn to recognize them and know when we are hearing them, we can begin to deal with them, first with honor and thanks, and then by reminding them their task is complete. Eventually, we can reassign them to a new task in helping us to bring our vision and purpose into the world.

Spirit, soul, and ego speak to us in very different ways and deliver very different kinds of messages. So how do we determine which voice we are hearing? Like anything else, it takes practice. As you step into the threshold, you will find your soul reflected to you in the natural world and speaking to you through your journaling. Spirit will speak to you in the quiet of meditation and the peaceful stillness of a starry night sky. The following triads will be helpful to understand the different ways ego, Spirit, and soul might show up:

- Ego uses fear to keep us stuck. Spirit inspires us to trust and soar. Soul dares us to feel the fear and move forward anyway.

- Ego wants a plan. Spirit works without a net. Soul craves the experience.

- Ego looks to the past for guidance. Spirit knows no time at all. Soul lives in dream time.

- Ego says, "What will the neighbors say?" Spirit says, "There are no 'others' for we are all one." Soul seeks its own story to tell.

- Ego says, "Take the job at the bank; it is secure and has good benefits." Spirit says, "Whatever work you chose, all will be provided." Soul says, "How can I deliver my deepest gifts to the world?"

- Ego asks, "What's in it for me?" and thinks small and short term. Spirit says, "We live in an abundant universe." Soul feels the satisfaction of bringing its deepest gifts into the world while knowing, in doing so, others will be served as well.

- Ego tells us there is no need to look because we would never want to leap anyway. Spirit implores us to dance on the edge and then to spread our wings and fly. Soul relishes the adventure of stepping into an uncertain future.

These ideas, particularly the ones about ego, are broad and should not be taken literally. The ego will change over time, and yours might have a different voice than the one speaking above. The goal is for ego to continue to learn from experiences with Spirit and soul, so that, eventually, ego is completely in their service.

Chapter 4: Severance

> ***Reflection question:*** *How is the voice of ego showing up for you as you contemplate this process of the hero's journey? What does it sound like? Feel like? Now, ask the same questions about the voices of Spirit and soul. If you knew you couldn't fail, no matter which voice you followed, what would you do?*

Finding our People

So far on our journey, we have received clues about our vision for the world and our soul's purpose. These are essential tools we will need to find our boon, but what kind of hero would stop there? In order to complete the hero's boon, we must find the way we are to employ our vision and purpose in the service of something bigger than ourselves. It's time to find our people. It's time to find how we are to serve in the world.

One of the valuable aspects of the process of severance is it can help us come to understand what is truly important in our lives. By stripping away all the clutter in our homes, schedules, and psyches, we begin to create space, both the physical and energetic kind and then purposefully decide how to use it. What will we create of our lives now that we have room? Who or what shall we serve?

Service brings vision and purpose into the world in a tangible way. There is a Native American practice of asking, when considering decisions of great importance, "How will this decision affect the seventh generation?" This question signifies a commitment to something more than satisfying the immediate needs of the individuals making the decision. Instead, it brings into consciousness the needs of a broader community, perhaps

Your Place in the World

even all humanity. This practice acknowledges that no matter how powerful one person's vision and sense of purpose might be, they must still be balanced by service to a higher ideal or a greater good.

When God spoke to Moses through the burning bush, God delivered the message that Moses' vision (freedom from bondage for the Hebrews) and purpose (to lead the Hebrews to the Promised Land) were implicitly in service to a particular people (the Hebrews and their future generations). Like all true heroes' boons, Moses did not find something meant to benefit him alone, though it did serve to bring meaning and direction to his life. He was given a vision and purpose so he could serve a greater cause.

Our vision and purpose are intrinsically linked to the way we are to serve in the world. If your current clues about your vision and purpose seem to lack something, it may be the energy of service. You can bring in the energy of service by asking questions like: "Who will my vision serve?" and "Who or what will be served if I demonstrated my purpose in the world?"

The same clues from our lives about our vision and purpose can be mined for more information about service. If we have been moved by the vision of a particular person, perhaps we are meant to serve in a similar way. Likewise, if our true identity never flourished due to inadequacies of the educational system we experienced, then perhaps we are meant to serve the children of today who are locked in a similar situation. Sometimes it can be painful to look into our past, so I invite you to be gentle with yourself as you do. Perhaps this idea of finding how you are to serve in the world will provide the inspiration and energy you need to begin what is often a difficult process.

Chapter 4: Severance

There are two additional points to be made about the idea of "our people" in relation to service. The first is that our particular people might not be people at all. Many of us are called to serve the other than human world of Mother Earth, her habitats, and the plants and animals living there. There is certainly no shortage of ways to serve the planet today, and if that is what calls to you, then that is where you should use your gifts. The second point is the people we return to at the end of this process might not be the people we are to serve. The severance could include the community we live in. This is not meant to imply we have to leave our family and friends in order to live a mythic life, but it is a suggestion that those who are closest to us are not necessarily those meant to receive our message.

The intention of service unites our vision and purpose. It is the glue holding them together. It is the completion of the trinity, the circle returning to itself. To serve a vision with our most precious soul's gifts is to return to our Creator, to touch immortality.

The way we are to serve in the world will be found at the intersection of our heartache and our bliss. There, at the place where our greatest sorrow meets our deepest joy, the voice of the ego will finally be silenced. It is at this juncture where, in answer to the question, *what are you willing to give,* we finally, completely, and without reservation say, *everything.* We will then know there is only one thing we can do, only one thing we were born to do, because we have reached the place where we simply can't do anything else. We will know what it means to be human and simultaneously divine. As we stand on this holy ground, we will know we are home at last—we have found our people—and they have found us.

Your Place in the World

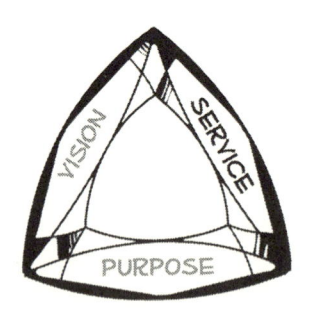

Mother Earth, Father Time, and a Daily Practice

As the first step on our journey, the process of severance begins to give us evidence the hero's boon serves the world as it serves us. Many of our modern ideas of success have not been particularly kind to Mother Earth. As our egos crave more material acquisitions in a misguided attempt to quiet our yearnings, our natural resources are being used up. When those material acquisitions fail to bring us the joy we seek, we discard them for the next new thing we believe will make us happy, and in the process our landfills become full. Humans continue to expand their footprint on the land with corporate farms and housing developments while species become extinct at a pace unprecedented in the history of the planet. Many of the very ideas coming up for examination in the process of severance may be the same ones that have contributed to so much planetary damage. Our souls crave another kind of life, a simpler way of living. Could it be there is a calling from the collective soul of the earth being felt in our own souls? Is the yearning we are feeling as individuals the individuation of a greater calling for change in the world itself?

If the goal is for the greater good of the human race and the earth it is hard to argue against the value of simplifying our lives.

Chapter 4: Severance

There are costs to our disposable society that have not yet been fully tallied. There is great value in empty spaces, whether we are talking about the extra room in our closets from not owning so many things or the blank spaces in our planning calendars to use for unstructured quiet time alone or with loved ones. Living a coherent life is good for our souls, and it might also be the answer to many of the challenges we are facing as a species.

Complexity has a cost. Our natural environment is paying the price of our need to have more, and we are passing this idea along to our children. As a parent, I feel the urge to give my children positive experiences, but only the future will reveal the cost of over filling our children's schedules. I wonder sometimes if children today have any space left in their days for just being a kid. In our loving attempt to protect them from harm, we keep them from playing in the woods or vacant lots in our neighborhoods. It is the unstructured time however, free from the supervision of adults, I most remember from my childhood. It is in these moments children first begin to hear the calling of their souls and find evidence of their particular gifts. Perhaps it is time for each of us to take our lives through a severance process, not just for our own sakes, but for the sake of future generations.

The process of severance is not a one-time event. At first, you may have a major house cleaning to do. Eventually, you will create a daily practice of releasing what no longer serves you. At some point, a formal process of severance may not be necessary, as you come to a place of singular vision. You begin to say "no," moment by moment, to what is not serving your soul's purpose and "yes" to what is.

Begin a practice of asking yourself this question as you ponder a decision you must make: How does this serve my soul? What would our lives look like if every decision we made, every word we spoke, and everything to which we committed our time and resources was made from this perspective? What if everyone in the world did this?

Each day we take one step closer to the final severance when we will leave this existence for the next one. In a way, all the severances we experience are nothing more than dress rehearsals for the final one. When we reach that time, how will we handle it? How will our children and our children's children remember us? Will we have regrets for the roads not taken, or will we feel joy for the way we followed our yearnings and lived our soul's purpose? Taking the time now to practice the process of severance will serve us well in the final passage into the next mysterious threshold.

Opening the Door and Stepping Through

Severance will take you into an in-between time that you could experience in many different ways. It might be frightening, or it might be exciting. It could be you feel a sense of freedom, or you might feel deep loss. It is possible you feel all of these things at once or nothing at all. Once you decide to move forward, the universe will begin to conspire with your soul to help your journey begin. You may feel irritation about things that never bothered you before. Your old life will feel more and more uncomfortable, and the pull of your yearning will grow stronger and more compelling. The time for the crossing of a threshold is close at hand. Know this: there is a greater love and power waiting for you on the other side of this experience. Let go and know all is well.

Activities

The following are designed to assit you in your severance process and help you uncover clues about how you are to serve in the world. Activity 1 and 2 are optional, but you will be doing activities in Chapter 6 that build on Activity 3 and 4, so don't skip those two.

At this stage, you are looking for clues, not final answers, so don't be concerned if what you find here doesn't make much sense to you. We will work with making sense of the clues in the Incorporation phase.

If you have difficulty with these activities, try rereading the section in the chapter titled *Finding our People*. You might also want to visit www.liveamythiclife.com where you will find worksheets you can download and use for these activities.

1. This is a severance activity that could take from 30 minutes to an entire weekend, depending on how thorough you are, but it might be something you have been meaning to do anyway.

   Clean out your closet. If you haven't worn it or used it in a year, maybe it's time to let it go. Donate the stuff you no longer need or that no longer serves the person you are becoming. Make a ritual out of the process by imagining each item you donate represents a part of your life you are letting go. The process will free up space, in your closet and in your consciousness, for the new energy waiting to come in. For an advanced activity, clean out your entire house or apartment. Have a garage sale or give away the things you no longer need.

2. This is a severance activity that will help you to separate the essential from the nonessential in your life. It will start

with a short reflection and then be spread over time, perhaps the rest of your life.

Spend some time thinking about this question: What would my life look like if I never made another decision without first asking "how will this serve my soul?" Try to go through one hour of a day without making any decisions or taking any actions until you have asked the question. After you have done this, expand it to one day, one week, or make it a permanent practice. Write about your experience with this activity in your journal.

3. This activity will help you to gather clues about how you are to serve in the world. It will take 30-60 minutes.

Step One: Turn in your journal to the pages you labeled: "Clues about my vision" and "Clues about my purpose." Spend time reflecting on what you have written there looking for clues about how you are meant to serve in the world. Look for patterns or places where you feel an emotional impact from reading your words. If nothing is coming to you, go back over the activities you used to find your clues about vision and purpose, and spend more time reading your journal notes. Think about how those you have called visionaries and wise elders have served in the world. Consider how the challenges you have dealt with in life might have given you clues about how you are meant to serve in the world.

Step Two: Turn to a clean page in your journal and write "Clues about how I am to serve in the world" at the top of the page. Begin to write down any ideas coming to you from Step One. Don't editorialize or criticize your answers or even try to make sense of them; there will be time for that later. For now, just capture anything coming into your mind or emerging from your heart as you consider this question.

Hint: If you are still having difficulty coming up with anything, try doing Activity 4 and then come back to Activity 3.

4. This activity is a way of doing severance. It might take you some time to complete, but it can be very powerful and is highly recommended.

Step One: Go back to look at the responses you gave to the following reflection question from this chapter:

Reflection question: Pause at this point and think about one particular aspect of your life. Maybe it's your job, a personal relationship, or an activity you engage in. It might also be a particular idea or attitude about life. Go with whatever comes to your mind first. Reflect on how you picked up the paper, added theat thing to your suitcase, or got on that bus—to borrow metaphors from the previous section. How does it look and feel to you now? What do you think it might it feel like to let it go? Do this for as many different parts of your life as you can think of. Then make some notes about this experience in your journal.

Step Two: Turn to a clean page in your journal and write these words at the top of the page: "These parts of my life do not support my emerging vision, purpose, and way of service."

Now, begin to list those aspects of your life that don't fit with the clues you have received about your hero's boon. Spend some time with this, perhaps spreading the activity out over several days, so you develop as complete a list as possible. Once you feel the list is complete, go back over it and circle the things that you are absolutely sure you are ready to release. Don't circle an item unless you are sure about letting it go.

Step Three: Once you have circled all the things on your list you are sure you are ready to let go of, take out another sheet of paper and transfer all of these items to it. (Hint: You might want to use a loose sheet, not one in your journal. The reason will become obvious shortly.) After transferring the items, use your imagination to create a ceremony where you will totally and finally release this second list. Perhaps you burn it in a fire. Maybe you put it through a paper shredder and then throw the pieces into the wind from the top of a cliff. Maybe you ceremonially read it to a trusted friend or loved one, tear it into bits, and release the bits into a river. Do whatever feels most powerful for you. Know that when the ceremony is complete, it is finished.

Step Four: If there are any items left on the original list, transfer them to another sheet of paper. These are things you think you might be ready to let go of but for one reason or another are not quite sure about yet. We'll call this the "Maybe List." Hold onto this list for a reflection question and an activity in Chapter Six.

For additional resources, including free downloadable worksheets you might find helpful in completing these activities, please visit www.liveamythiclife.com.

Chapter 5

The Threshold
Claiming what has always been

The hero has severed his ties with the life he has known and stepped completely into the threshold. In the threshold, the hero will be tested, and it is here that the boon may finally be claimed.

> *No man or woman, standing at the edge of their own inner pool of darkness, is exempt from the wish to pass by this stage, to find a safe, dry land bridge and walk across. We intuit in those waters the potentialities and dreams of a lifetime, but, finding them hidden by the strangely irrational depth of our own fear, we are not sure they are worth the grief.*
>
> - David Whyte

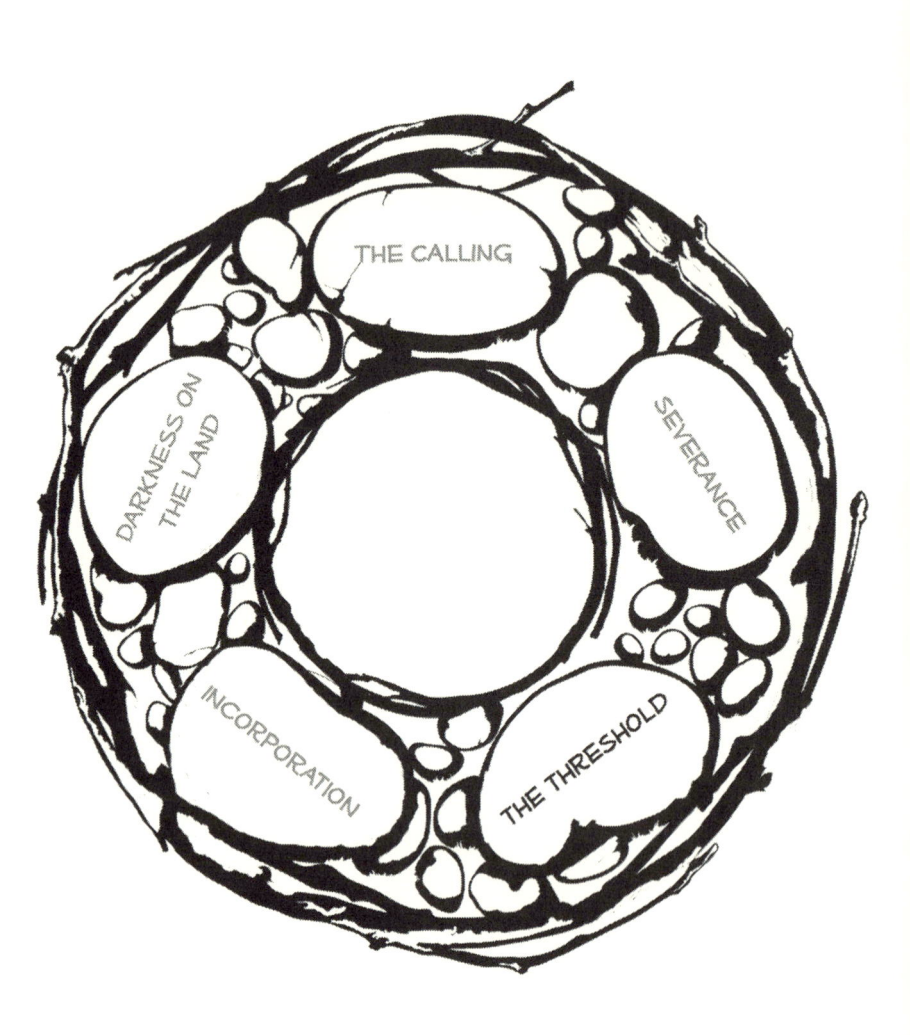

- THE CALLING
- SEVERANCE
- THE THRESHOLD
- INCORPORATION
- DARKNESS ON THE LAND

Chapter 5

Letter from Home: I believe in you. Always have, always will. But who believes in you more? The entire universe! The entire cosmos is rushing forth to meet you—your heart, your intention, your love—and provide what you desire at this very moment! Piece of cake!

Solo Time

When I stepped out of the circle of stones on that August morning, I stepped into another world. It was the moment for which I had spent months preparing. As I shouldered my pack, I thought about the things it contained. There were the basic survival supplies: a sleeping bag, ground cloth, tarp, and a few articles of clothing. I had taken a three day supply of water, the most important thing I would need, to my solo site the day before. The journal I had begun to write in three months prior was stuffed somewhere in the pack along with my flute, a book of Rumi's poems, and my watch, which I wouldn't wear again until I returned. Most precious of all, I carried the bag of cards my wife sent along, one for each day of my vision quest. I had begun opening them two days before, on my birthday, and knew there was another one waiting for me for each day until I was on my way back to her.

Your Place in the World

As I walked away from base camp, I thought about the many people in my life who were walking with me. My wife, Leslie, who had loved and supported me through the years we had been together and who was burning a candle for me back home, a candle she lit when I left and would not extinguish until I returned to her. I thought about my children and wondered what stories they would tell about their Dad in the years to come. I thought about all the people in my spiritual community who had prayed for me in the days leading up to my vision quest and who were still praying for my safe return. And there were the two guides, Michael and Linda, who I had only met a few days before and yet already, seemed like old friends. They were there at the edge of this threshold to give me the final pieces of instruction and advice I would need for my journey. They had shown me how to stay safe in the wilderness, how to create shelter, and how to become clearer about my intention for my solo time.

While there were so many people with me in spirit, I was taking this walk alone. I had never spent three days in total solitude before, let alone in the wilderness. I knew my buddy wouldn't be far away and my solo site was only a twenty minute hike from base camp, yet I still felt the growing isolation. At the same time, I felt the wilderness welcoming me. It started tentatively, like one might feel when entering a stranger's house for the first time, but with each step I took, I could feel a greater level of acceptance from the rocks and trees. I began to feel I knew this place as well as my own house. The more I accepted the land, the more it accepted me, and by the time I reached my solo site, I knew I had found a new kind of home.

For the next three days and nights, I had no human companionship. Although I had ample water to drink, I took no food.

Chapter 5: The Threshold

I slept on Mother Earth with only a ground cloth, a sleeping pad, and my sleeping bag between us. If the weather turned bad, I could create enough shelter to stay dry by putting up the small tarp I brought along; otherwise, I fell asleep looking at the stars. Although the guides had given me a few ideas about some simple ceremonies I could do during my time alone, I had no definite plans. With no watch and no mealtimes to frame my day, I kept time by the passing of the sun, the moon, and the stars.

When I think back on that time, I remember I was sometimes bored. I also recall having moments of deep clarity when it seemed as if everything I wanted to know was being revealed to me in a single moment. It was like a dream I was experiencing while awake. Without the attachment to my normal routine and surroundings, I felt anchorless but somehow also deeply rooted in a new world, a new reality.

As the days passed, I felt myself slowing down. The high altitude and lack of food kept me moving slowly; I spent a lot of time just sitting. This slowness gave me time to think and to observe. I watched the sky, the sparrows in the brush around me, the ants scurrying in the sand, the distant hills and mountains. I sensed they were watching me, too.

I left my human companions behind when I walked away from base camp, but now I had a different kind of companionship. The sky, the sparrows, the rocks, the hills: all these were my friends, and I spoke with them, telling them my story while trying to hear theirs. The rocks bore silent yet comforting witness to my tears as I grieved for the family I missed so deeply. The trees held me and heard the conversations I needed to have with my loved ones. I made peace with my demons, at least some of them, under the watchful and supporting gaze of a huge towering boulder, my sentinel and personal totem for the experience.

On the first day of my solo, I faced the south and thought of my childhood and my own children. I thought about the boy I had once been and wondered if he still lived in me. I remembered being a kid who loved exploring, whether it was exploring the mountains in North Carolina or a coral reef in the Florida Keys, and I realized there was still some explorer in me. I thought about how some of that kid was reflected back to me in the eyes of my own children, and I gave thanks for the blessings they are in my life. That night, as the sun was setting, I built a small fire and ceremonially called in my Loyal Soldier. I thanked him for his service but let him know the child I once was no longer needed protection. I asked him to take on a new task, to help me to stay on the path I was setting and to remind me when I was veering off course.

On the second day, I faced the west and thought about all the loves of my life, and in particular, my wife Leslie. I thought about the gift of love and all the lessons I've learned along the way through my relationships. During the afternoon, I constructed a ceremonial death lodge. Two large rocks, close in proximity, became walls, and I placed some sticks across the top for the semblance of a roof. That evening I crawled inside, lit a candle at the entrance, and invited anyone I had ever known to visit me as if I were a man about to die. As the spirits of people from my life came, I asked for and gave forgiveness and said my goodbyes. That night, after leaving the lodge, I felt like I really could die. Everything I needed to do had been done.

On the third day, I faced the north and thought about all the wise elders in my life—parents, teachers, bosses, and other mentors—who had selflessly given a part to themselves to me.

Chapter 5: The Threshold

I thanked them all and made peace with those from whom I had felt estranged. I reflected on the role each had played in my life and also on the wise elder I was becoming myself. On that particular day, I spent time reflecting on my relationship with my father and, in the process, came to see the kind of father I am, with all my strengths and shortcomings. In the afternoon I constructed a circle of stones I would sit in all night, and I began to think about my return to base camp the following morning.

At sunset I stepped into my stone circle. It was large enough to sit and walk around in, but not large enough for me to lie down, thereby removing the temptation to sleep. I stayed awake all night, watching the sun set in the west and the stars circle around Polaris. After many hours in my circle, I began to see a glow coming from the east. Although the night had been long, it didn't seem time for the sunrise; nevertheless, it gave me hope. I watched, chanting, "Come on sun, come on sun!" I was cold and tired, and, after three days without food, more than ready to pack up and head back to the base camp breakfast I knew would be waiting. "Come on sun!"

I watched as the eastern sky continued to brighten. The stars, which had been shining intensely, began to dim until there were no more to be seen in the east. Slowly, the sky lightened, and then the faintest sliver of glowing orb peaked above the ridgeline. A moment later I began to see its shape. It was then the coyotes began to howl, for they knew what I was just beginning to realize: the light was coming, not from the rising sun but from a brilliantly shining, nearly-full moon. I laughed at myself and settled in for the rest of the long, cold night.

Hours later, when the sun rose, I asked this question: "Am I Peacemaker?" I received an answer: *Yes*. I felt glad in the knowing, but something was missing from the experience. It felt as if something was yet to be revealed. Looking back, I now realize I should have listened more closely to the coyotes. In their cries was a warning not to take the messages too literally or interpret them too soon. The hero must return from the threshold, bringing his vision to the world, before the boon can be truly appreciated and understood.

As the sun rose fully into the eastern sky, I stood playing a song of joy and triumph on my flute. Its notes echoed off the rocks and canyon walls and came back to me as confirmation of the completion of this phase of my journey. It was time to return from the threshold.

The Threshold

The threshold is an energetic space—a pause—between the release of the severance and the beginning of the incorporation. It is the cocoon stage between the caterpillar and the butterfly, when all form breaks down so a new and more beautiful one can be created. The threshold is a piece of white paper, a blank canvas waiting for the painter to begin.

Threshold is emptiness and dreamtime. In the threshold, the veil between the physical world and the world of the imagination is the thinnest and is often and easily parted, revealing the wonder hiding behind it, as well as the dragons. We should not be surprised by what we see and hear in the threshold. The rocks and trees might have something to tell us, if we take the time to listen. Why shouldn't we learn from the birds in this place? Don't they understand the cycle of the seasons, the turning of the day, the fragility of life? The threshold is a time of listening, feeling, and experiencing.

Chapter 5: The Threshold

In the myths, the severance occurs at the point the hero enters the dark forest, crawls into the cave, or dives into a lake. The threshold is the experience that follows. Jonah's time in the belly of the great fish, Noah's experience in the ark, and Odysseus' journey home can all be seen as threshold experiences.

Threshold is also often represented by a desert experience. Many of the founders of the world's great spiritual traditions began their ministries after a time in the desert. The perfect example is Jesus' battle with Satan during his forty-day experience at the start of his ministry. Just as Jesus wrestled with his devil in the threshold, so too must we. The threshold can be a time of facing not only our fears but also the false prophets who would tempt us to settle for less than the full realization of our life's potential.

The desert itself is a perfect metaphor for the threshold experience. The desert is a land of big sky and wide-open spaces. Seemingly desolate and devoid of life to the casual observer, the desert is actually teeming with life, if you know where and how to look. The heat of the desert causes one to slow down, and when we do, we notice the smaller details. Likewise, the threshold is about slowing down enough to pay attention. The smallest of details becomes important: the ant busy in the sand at our feet, the fly buzzing by our head, the sparrow in the tree above us; all have a message for us if we stop and take notice.

The threshold time is often associated with the time of day when the sun is beginning to set. The shadows grow longer at sunset, and we have to squint just to focus our eyes. It's a magical time of dreams and deep imagination. As the sun sets, or as we walk deeper into a dark wood, our sense of seeing with our eyes becomes less and less useful until finally, we can't trust our eyes at all. Other senses take over, and our imaginations awaken. We enter a time between waking and sleeping, where everything seems more possible than in the full light of the day. This is the land of the soul.

The threshold is a portal to the underworld. This is not the underworld some of us picture as a place where our souls spend eternity if we have not followed a prescribed path during our lives on earth; rather, this is the land of the psyche into which all of us must dive if we are to be fully initiated into our own soul. There is a reason why the underworld journey is a common path for the heroes in the stories: the myths are telling us we must come face to face with our souls and bring forth what we find there if we are to become complete adults.

The power of the threshold lies in the state of mind it elicits. The threshold represents a place of all possibility—a place of magic and mystery. By deliberately stepping into that state of mind, we help create the opportunity for greater clarity about our boon. Stripped of the world's expectations and our own, we are left with nothing but the true essence of our being. We are now in a place where we can engage in deep listening to hear what the soul has to tell us.

We could learn something here from the stories of heroes and their journeys. While we don't necessarily need to go on a vision quest, we can find other ways to integrate this in-between time into our lives. We can learn to value the silence, rather than automatically trying to fill it. We can learn to appreciate the stillness to be found within the activity of life, the times when we feel a need to turn within and reflect. Our Western culture has tended to turn its back on stillness; perhaps it is time to welcome it in.

I experienced a threshold in my life several years before I went on my vision quest. A series of events led my wife and me,

Chapter 5: The Threshold

each in our own way, to become clear we were supposed to move to another city. So, in spite of not having a job offer in the new city or any clear idea why we were supposed to move there, we packed up our children and our belongings and moved. As we began making the preparations to leave our previous home, one door after another closed behind us, insuring we couldn't turn around in fear. I wrapped up my business dealings, our house sold quickly, and we found a place to live in the new town.

For the first month after arriving, I was in a state of mind unlike any I had experienced before. Since I didn't yet fully understand why I had been brought to this new place, I entered each day with a sense of expectation. Perhaps that day would be the one where I would find out why I had moved to this new town. Each day became a day of discovery. Each encounter with another person became an opportunity to receive a new gift. Each experience was met with curiosity and receptivity. In time, I found a job and settled into something like a normal routine, but I often think about that period of my life. I try to recall the feeling of wonder I carried with me all the time and I attempt to bring some of that attitude into my current life.

I don't know how long you will be in the threshold. For some of us, there is a tendency to want to rush through the threshold to the other side. We want to complete the cycle as quickly as we can. The woods are much too dark and deep, and the idea of warming ourselves by the fire of our new vision compels us to push through as quickly as possible. We gather the messages together, interpreting them as we go, and begin assembling the puzzle before we have all the pieces. What we are left with ends up being a confusing mess, so we think the threshold was a failure. Take your time in this place and know the opportunity to interpret the messages will come later.

Your Place in the World

> ***Reflection question:*** *What would your day look like if, before rising from bed, you affirmed: "Today is the day for which I have been born"? How might that affect your outlook on life, the passion with which you greet your loved ones, or the dedication you bring to your work? What if each day was not only the day for which you had been born but also your last day on earth? How then might you live your life?*

Fasting, Solitude, and Exposure

There are three elements always present with ceremonies like the vision quest, no matter what culture or time period from which they originate. The first is fasting. On a vision quest, the participant fasts from eating food for a period of days. Some indigenous people believe true wisdom is held in the belly and it is difficult for us to hear and receive that wisdom if our stomachs are full. Emptying the stomach by fasting creates space for new ideas and visions to fill the empty space, much like the severance creates space in our lives. The hunger in the belly is also a constant reminder of the hunger in the soul. Going without food for a few days is a small price to pay if the goal is finding a vision to serve our people.

Fasting comes in many forms. Not only can we fast from food, we can fast from watching television, eating sweets, or drinking coffee. We can also fast from holding particular kinds of thoughts. If we have determined we want to give up thinking badly about a coworker, maybe we could first try fasting from those thoughts for a period of days. Fasting could be thought of as a continuation of the severance process. If there is a particular

Chapter 5: The Threshold

activity, thought, or behavior you have decided to release in the severance process, then you might commit now to fast from it as you enter the threshold. Who knows, you might just find you have no desire to go back to that old habit once you return.

The second key element is solitude. In the myths the hero might start his or her journey with a band of compatriots but usually must part from them in order to complete the journey. This time in solitude has been a part of every spiritual leader, saint, and mystic's journey. There is a need, it seems, for us to take time apart in order to more fully engage with our people.

On a vision quest, the participant also starts in the company of others. We need other human beings to hear us and to reflect our stories back to us, but we also need to be alone. We need time with our own thoughts, and we need the experience of being alone with ourselves. Solitude brings quiet with it, and the quiet allows us to better hear the voice of soul.

Solitude is something few of us get enough of. Few places offer respite from assault by television screens and computer monitors streaming their messages to us. Many of us are plugged into the Internet all the waking hours of our day. Our cell phones keep us in constant contact. Unlike many of our ancestors who had to go out of their way to have human contact, we often have to make a special effort to find solitude.

Solitude is essential to hearing the voice of the soul. We don't have to go away for days to get it, either. Spending a few minutes every day just sitting alone with your thoughts away from the television, telephone, and computer is a good start. If you do nothing else I recommend in this book, if you take no other idea away from this experience, I pray you will add regularly scheduled time in solitude to your life.

The third key element is exposure. On the vision quest, this means exposure to the natural elements such as sun, wind, heat, cold, rain, and snow. In indigenous cultures, the person going on a quest often did so naked and without any tools or shelter except perhaps a robe or blanket. In a modern vision quest, the possessions are nearly as limited, at least in comparison to our normal lives. Typically, the participant will sleep on the ground under a small tarp but without a tent. The comforts of home are left behind, and the natural world becomes the teacher. The wind can speak, if its voice is not being blocked out by human-made sounds. Likewise, the cold and rain have something to teach us about ourselves if we are fully present to their wisdom.

How else might we bring the element of exposure into our threshold time? How about exposure to new ideas, cultures, or spiritual beliefs? Wandering through a library or an art gallery can be just as revealing as wandering in the woods if we view the experience as an adventure into unknown lands. We can invite the books or works of art to call to us, and then spend some time with those that get our attention, observing what is revealed. Going into a part of town we rarely visit, eating food we have never tried, or visiting a church, temple, or other religious center we have never attended can all serve in this function of exposure. Our soul responds to these activities, and we will come away with new insights about ourselves and our lives.

Stating your Name and Stepping Through the Portal

On the way to the threshold time, you have received some clues about the three components of the hero's boon: vision, purpose,

Chapter 5: The Threshold

and service. You have decided to release some things no longer serving you: attitudes, self images, and some of the stories you have been carrying around about yourself. The portal is just too narrow for those things to fit through. Perhaps you have met your Loyal Soldier and let him know his mission has been accomplished and a new one may soon be revealed. Now the time has come to finally step through the portal and into the threshold.

The question, then, is how to begin? It is helpful, as at the passing of any milestone, to mark it with a ceremony. This is particularly true when stepping into a threshold time. Many people light candles or incense to indicate a passing from one world into another. The Native American practice of smudging with sage smoke is also very adaptable to the marking of a threshold. Drawing a line in the sand and then stepping across it is a simple way to mark this passing. As with any ceremony, the form is not nearly as important as the intent, so whatever ceremony you use, do so with an intention of respect and a level of mystery.

Portals into thresholds can occur wherever we look, and each time we cross one, we have another opportunity to mark the occasion. We cross a portal when we get out of bed in the morning, when we sit down to our breakfast, and when we leave the house for work or school. We come to portals throughout our day when we enter a room for a meeting or pick up the phone to call a client. How about those moments when we confront a particularly vexing challenge or a difficult person? These are opportunities to cross a portal as well. Each time we are making a shift from one path to another, we are presented with an opportunity to view the new place we are moving to as a time in the threshold. By seeing those moments as if we are

Your Place in the World

stepping across a portal and into a threshold, we are signaling to our minds, hearts, and souls we are open to whatever guidance might be available for us.

It isn't a requirement to physically go into the wilderness to have a threshold experience. What is required is the right frame of mind. We begin to create the right frame of mind with the severance process. We continue to deepen the process when we perform a ceremony at the start of the threshold. These two steps help to create the open mind that serves us well as we begin to wander about in search of more clues about our boon.

There is an ancient idea that when we know something's name, we understand its nature. When Moses asked the burning bush, "Who shall I say sent me," he was asking God, "Who are you? What is your nature?" In the Native American tradition, the young person returning from the vision quest is given a new name that describes the kind of person they are, as demonstrated by the kind of experience they had on their quest. This new name describes their true nature. When you and I start conversations with someone we haven't met before, we usually do so by first introducing ourselves by stating our name. We also trade information about our professions, providing further information, in our own culturally acceptable way, about the nature of one another. As we stand at the portal to the threshold, it would, therefore, be appropriate to introduce ourselves to this new place by stating our name.

But what name shall we use? Will it be the name we were given by our parents, or would another name be more appropriate for this moment? So far on our hero's journey, we have begun to discover an identity for ourselves that is less influenced by the ego and more influenced by Spirit and soul. Our new identity, which is actually our true identity, is inspired by our

Chapter 5: The Threshold

vision, grounded in our purpose, and connected to our way of serving in the world. Now is the time to take on a new name that reflects this identity. We will call this name our "soul name." Activity 3 at the end of this chapter will help you to formulate your soul name.

When we say our soul name, we are setting an intention. We are not asking for something to occur, nor are we asking if this name is accurate. Instead, we are stating, with power and conviction, that this is who we truly are. When we speak our soul name, it should feel like a bit of a stretch, but it should be believable, as well. The threshold provides a blank canvas upon which to try out this new understanding about ourselves and, in so doing, it provides a testing ground for this name. As we spend time in the threshold, we will have experiences that may refute our name, affirm it, or deepen our understanding of it. For now, however, we create our name as best we understand it. Then, as we stand at the edge of the portal, at the edge of our world, we will speak our name into the wind so all may bear witness.

The following poem by Mary Oliver speaks to this idea of stepping through a portal and into a threshold time while listening for our name.

> *One day you finally knew*
> *what you had to do, and began,*
> *though the voices around you*
> *kept shouting*
> *their bad advice-*
> *though the whole house*
> *began to tremble*
> *and you felt the old rug*

> *at your ankles.*
> *"Mend my life!"*
> *each voice cried.*
> *But you didn't stop.*
> *You knew what you had to do,*
> *though the wind pried*
> *with its stiff fingers*
> *at the very foundations,*
> *though their melancholy*
> *was terrible.*
> *It was already late*
> *enough, and a wild night,*
> *and the road full of fallen*
> *branches and stones.*
> *But little by little,*
> *as you left their voices behind,*
> *the stars began to burn*
> *through the sheets of clouds,*
> *and there was a new voice*
> *which you slowly recognized as your own,*
> *that kept you company*
> *as you strode deeper and deeper*
> *into the world,*
> *determined to do*
> *the only thing you could do-*
> *determined to save*
> *the only life you could save.*[1]

We must learn to trust our own voice. So, speak your soul name with power and conviction. Speak it with pride. Hear

Chapter 5: The Threshold

yourself and allow this new understanding of the beautiful human being you were born to be to resonate from the crown of your head, through your solar plexus, and down into the very ground upon which you stand. Listen to this new voice which, as Mary Oliver says, you will "slowly recognize as your own."

Trouble at the Border[2]

For many, the hero's journey ends at the call. The hero ignores the call or, worse yet, acknowledges it but refuses to do anything about it. For some, their call is a precious jewel, a personal dance with the psyche, or a cross to bear. Still others get stuck at the severance, at the very edge of their bliss, never quite willing to enter fully into the dance with soul. They sit like adolescent wallflowers watching people around them enjoy their lives and create things of lasting value. Their own personal heroes are men and women who have risked it all to live a dream or serve the greater good, yet they fail to recognize those same heroic possibilities within themselves.

It is easy to get stuck at the portal between severance and threshold. If our fears haven't gotten our attention before, we surely will hear them now. We all have what it takes to live our dreams. There is a reason we are feeling the urge to take this journey and, while we can't know precisely where the path will take us, we can trust our inner yearning to begin. We carry the source of the yearning within us, and the path to its fulfillment lies there as well.

I experienced my own fear at the portal to my threshold in the form of an imaginary bear. About a month before my vision quest, I began thinking about bears—and not in a good way. Even though I grew up camping and hiking in the bear country of western North Carolina without ever seeing one, let alone being frightened of them, I started worrying I might have to deal with a bear on my vision quest. I would fall asleep at night with them on my mind, and sometimes they would show up in my dreams, but I did my best to put the fear aside, and I didn't let it stop me from making the journey.

On the afternoon I had the encounter with the trout, we had a council where I shared this fear. You can imagine my relief when our lead guide, Michael, told me there weren't any bears in the White Mountains where we would be camping. Then, he pulled a lanyard from around his neck to which a small carved stone bear was attached. He explained to me that for some Native American cultures the bear is the totem animal of the west, which is the land of the soul. I had been called on this journey by the yearnings of my soul, and my ego was sending warning signs about taking the trip. The only bear I was going to encounter on my vision quest was the one I would find by looking inside—but that was scary enough.

As we stand at the edge of the threshold, it is natural to feel some fear. We can take heart though, for, as is often the case in the myths, helpful spirits will appear at the gate bearing amulets and protections against the demons and dragons we will face. Who are these spirits? They are many and varied. The spirits are the people who show up with a kind word just when things seem to be going against us. They might be books we read (perhaps this one) and songs we hear that give us new ideas, lift our hearts, or inspire us to forge ahead into the night. They may be the people who have gone before us and left a trail to follow. Some may receive guidance from listening to animals, birds, or the earth itself. All these guides have something to teach us. If we ask our questions and speak our fears, there will

Chapter 5: The Threshold

be an answer. The world loves the hero, and all the powers of the universe are here to support us on our hero's journey.

This does not mean we should completely ignore our fears. Fear can teach us and strengthen us. As mentioned in the chapter on severance, the ego frequently uses fear to maintain control, so fear is often a good sign we are on the right track. Besides, what kind of hero's journey would it be without some serious fear? People who have faced their fears and moved through them are the ones who inspire us. It is right that we perceive obstacles standing between where we are and the fulfillment of our yearning, but these fears are only perceptions. They have no power themselves; they have only the power we give them in our minds.

Fear can take many forms. What form does your fear take? What name do you give to it? My personal demon has the name Financial Failure. It sometimes shows up with its cousin, Not Enough, or will appear clothed in the guise of Responsibility and Taking-Care-of-My-Family, but, at its root it is a fear about not measuring up in the eyes of the world. For me, facing and slaying that dragon required that I get to a place where I released my attachment to keeping things in my material world the way they had always been. Learning to trust that the universe will always supply all I need enabled me to step deeply into my own hero's journey and wholeheartedly answer the yearning of my soul. It is a war that never seems completely won. We each fight the battles one at a time, gaining a little territory here or a strategic hill there. All the while, our souls ask us to face the fear and move forward anyway.

In an ironic and strange way, our fears can give us wonderful gifts. By facing them, we reveal who we are at the depth of our souls. By conquering them, we discover the gifts we are to give to the world. By dancing with them and then letting them go, we can learn what they have to teach us and, by example, lead others in their struggles.

There is a power greater than any fear we might have: it is the power of love. Love can overcome the fear of anything. We have to be in love with our dreams. We have to be in love with the life we are visualizing for ourselves. We have to be in love with the project we long to complete, the relationship we want to begin, the work we imagine doing.

The path we are walking is, in fact, the path of love. We can love our dreams into being. The source of our yearning is calling out from our souls in love, drawing our attention and our bodies toward it. Our dreams need us the same way we need our dreams. Without the energy of our minds and bodies, our dreams cannot come true. Without our dreams, we are hollow shells, empty vessels floating through life rather than fully living as we are all meant to do. When we consider our hopes and dreams, the question to ask ourselves may not be, "How badly do I want it?" but rather, "How deeply do I love it?"

> *Reflection question:* Are any fears showing up at this point on your journey? See if you can name and describe them. Can you also begin to see, if only just barely, the benefits of pushing past them? If the fears seem to be taking up a lot of your thoughts, try focusing instead on the possibilities beyond them.

The Time in the Threshold

Now is the time to take one small step into the unknown. The key to the next phase of the journey is to give your mind the

Chapter 5: The Threshold

day off. Your rational mind has brought you far and will have a role to play in the incorporation phase to come, but for now, you will be better served if you put figuring the experience out aside for a while.

It is here in the threshold that your soul name will be tested. Are you really serious about the vision you are beginning to see? Are you ready to accept the purpose you are feeling called toward? Are you committed to the life of service you have begun to imagine? To say we wish to change the way we have been living our life is one thing—it is quite another to actually do so. While you have been gathering clues along your path, the threshold is where the hero's boon is really found; because it is here that it will be alchemically transformed from mere concepts and sentiments into a new way of being.

The truths we feel in our bodies, hearts, and souls, rather than the truths we speak with our tongues, have the most power. Although we know they are real, it may be difficult for us to prove it. Likewise, a path we can see from one end to another, including where it emerges from the woods, has little power to engage and inspire us. It is the great mysteries in life, not the answers, which keep us moving forward and make life interesting. The threshold is a time of deep mystery, and it takes strength of spirit to meet the mystery on its own terms rather than demanding it provide us with a well-marked map to guide us along the way.

The threshold experience asks us to have faith that each step will become clearer as we take the one immediately in front of us. I was exposed to this concept at an early age. When I was a child, my family used to spend our vacations camping near a river, where one of my favorite activities was walking on the stones that just barely rose up above the surface in the shallow

Your Place in the World

areas. It was a challenge to see how far out into the river I could walk without getting my feet wet. When I stood on the bank and looked out, I couldn't plan my route more than a few stones at a time. But I learned that as I stepped into the river, I'd begin to see other stones on which I could step. Sometimes they were barely visible at the surface of the water and impossible to see until I was right next to them, but they were always there. A route appeared as I committed to taking the path.

Working your way through the threshold will be a lot like walking on the stones in the river. You may only be able to see the first step or two, but if you want to cross the river, you are going to have to trust that the stones you need will be there when you need them. The thing to do is take the first step, then another, and another. Soon you will recognize how far you have come. Along the way, you might also learn, as I did as a child, that it's not all that bad to fall in and get your feet wet!

While we may be called into the threshold by a particular question or yearning, once we are there it is helpful to remember that which seemed to call us is but an echo of the true reason for being there, a ruse our soul has employed to get our attention. The quicker we let go of the need to understand the literal meaning of the calling, the quicker we come to know the true purpose of our journey. We should use the calling to guide us while maintaining a certain sense of detachment from fully understanding it. Our calling might be like the first enticing rock in the river was for me as a boy. We step forward and allow the next stones to rise up to guide our feet.

If we have done our severance work well and are stepping into this time as naked and vulnerable as our hearts can bear, we can expect to find answers in the threshold. But it is important we not have any preconceived ideas about the form those answers might

Chapter 5: The Threshold

take. We should be open to the universe and allow its power to work its magic. We can never know for sure how and when guidance will show up; all we can really do is prepare and wait, and then take the steps forward as they reveal themselves.

As you wander about, you might start to get messages from the environment. You can dismiss them or accept them into the realm of the psyche and allow them to begin to work on you. Does the bird in the tree have something to tell you? Is the wind calling your name or perhaps trying to offer you a new one? What does the creek next to you have to share about the question you have been wrestling with? By suspending your disbelief, you will allow the imagination to work and nature to serve as a mirror to what you hold within you.

The elements of the natural world are effective mirrors to our own inner, inborn natures. Watching a soaring hawk might tell us to set our soul free to soar on its own wings. Experiencing the peaceful beauty of a sunset can reflect back to us the peace and beauty lying within our own hearts. Sitting in the presence of a centuries-old oak tree might remind us how strength can come from the smallest of ideas.

When we commune with the wild world, we discover our own wildness. We touch the great mystery that is our life, the great unfolding that is the path we are invited to walk. As we surrender our old lives by stepping through severance and into the threshold, we step into the mystery of the unknown, trusting that the power of grace will carry us safely to the other side.

When I talk with people about doing soul work in nature, they sometimes reveal fear about being out in the woods alone. While being in the woods requires a different set of safety precautions than walking down a city street, it is no more dangerous. Even so, some people simply refuse to look past their fear.

What is it they fear? I believe it is rooted in a fear of looking deeply into the mirror nature provides to our souls. The anxiety we feel when we walk into the dark woods is connected to our own fear of looking into the dark places inside us. While there is nothing behind those trees that wants to harm us, our souls might have something to tell us that could seriously challenge our current way of living. If we feel fear of nature, it might be time to question what it is we fear within ourselves.

The threshold experience is the process of holding our souls up to a mirror and looking deeply into the reflection there. While we may seek the world around us for answers, we do so with the intention of finding the meaning that lies within us; for truly, that is the only place we will find our answers. The tug outward is actually a tug inward toward our true home. It is a constant and unfolding process: we look within to find our gift to give to the outer world, which, in turn, becomes another mirror for us to look within once more, to find a greater gift, and on and on. It is not a circle so much as it is an ever-evolving, upwardly progressing spiral. We are always learning and growing.

> *Reflection question:* How could you purposefully create threshold moments in your day? Where might you begin to insert pauses through which your soul can begin to be heard?

Claiming the Boon

The hero travels far from his home in search of his boon. He has adventures, meets challenges, and, along the way discovers the secrets of his soul. But when does the journey end? How

Chapter 5: The Threshold

does the hero know it is time to leave the threshold and return to his people? The hero might very well continue to journey for the rest of his life unless he does one crucial and important thing: claim the boon. Like the young boy-who-would-be-king Arthur, grasping the sword by the hilt and pulling it from the stone, the hero must reach out, put his hands on the boon, and call it his own.

It might seem an obvious step, but many stumble at this task. We can have all kinds of spiritually revealing experiences. We can heal our wounds, discover our purpose, and find our vision, but until we claim these things as our own, they will be nothing more than moments we remember and stories we tell.

In the myths, the hero will often face one final test on his way out of the threshold. In this test, he must prove he is the rightful possessor of the boon he now carries. You will also be tested. The world will present plenty of tests that question the validity of your experiences and the message you carry, and until and unless you claim your boon, you will not have the strength to face them.

As you stand at the return portal and prepare to leave the threshold, speak your name once more. This might be the same name you spoke as you entered the threshold, or it might be another version you have discovered as you walked your path. Listen deeply and critically to your words. Do they resonate for you? Do you believe them, or at least believe that you believe them? You are claiming a new identity for yourself, so chose well, but don't worry too much at this point about how this new person will show up in the world; that is the work of the incorporation period to follow. For now, claim you hero's boon by standing once again at the edge of the world and speaking your name for all to hear.

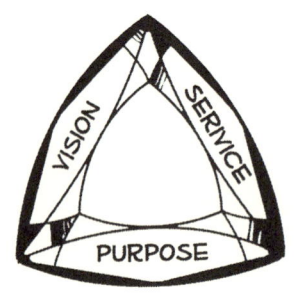

Heading for Home

After sunrise on the fourth morning after leaving base camp, I packed up my few belongings, gently dismantled my stone circle, and hiked back down the canyon to meet the rest of my group and enjoy a warm meal. It was time to begin the return home and to undertake the process of understanding what home really meant.

When I returned to base camp, the guides were waiting there with wide smiles and open arms. I stepped back into the stone circle for another blessing of sage smoke and love, welcomed back as a returning hero with stories to tell and gifts to share. After we all passed back through, we dismantled the circle, leaving no trace of its existence, symbolically closing the portal behind us. It was time to begin the incorporation.

Activities

Now that you have read about threshold, try experiencing it by doing one or more of these activities. Of all of these, it will be most important to do number 2 before moving on to the next chapter.

1. This activity will help you find ways to create small thresholds in your daily life. It will take about an hour but could be stretched over a day or more. Do at least Steps One and Two, but for an even richer experience, add Step Three.

   Step One: Find a place where you can spend at least 30 minutes of uninterrupted time by yourself. It might be a comfortable chair in your house, a park bench, a museum, or any other place that feels right to you. Before starting, make a mental note of your general mood, tension and anxiety levels, etc. Once you settle into this spot, avoid doing anything that would engage your mind. Don't read, don't watch television, and don't work on your grocery list; just sit. Allow your mind to wander where it wants to go. If you like, get up and walk around, but don't do so with any intention of getting anywhere; just aimlessly wander. If a little voice inside your head starts to complain by saying, "This is a big waste of time," simply reply with, "Thank you for sharing, but I'm giving myself this gift right now and will get back to you later." At the end of the time you allowed for this part of the activity, make another mental note about your mood, tension and anxiety levels, etc.

Your Place in the World

Step Two: You can do this step immediately after completing Step One, later the same day, or the following day. Take out your journal and answer these questions:

- Did your mind complain at all about "wasting time?" Were you able to convince it to leave you alone for a bit?

- What kind of thoughts came up for you during Step One? Anything having to do with the work you have been doing in this book? If so, make a note of those ideas.

- What differences do you notice in your mood, tension and anxiety levels, or overall sense of peace and well-being between the start of Step One and its end?

- Can you see any benefit in doing this kind of activity on a regular basis? Are you willing to make a commitment to yourself to do so now?

Step Three: Look back at the section in this chapter titled, *Fasting, Solitude, and Exposure*. Think about ways you might expand the experience in Steps One and Two by adding one or more of these elements. For example, you could fast from eating while spending a day in solitude wandering around at a nature park. Or you could take a trip without an agenda to a town or city you haven't previously visited. Use your imagination and enjoy the experience.

2. This activity will help you with finding your soul name. It will take anywhere from 30-60 minutes and is important for completing the work in the following chapter.

Chapter 5: The Threshold

Step One: Turn back to the page in your journal you labeled, "Clues about My Purpose," and spend a few minutes reading what you have written there. Now, knowing your purpose describes your essential nature, fill in the blank in the following phrase with the word or words that describes the person you are:

"I am a _____ man/woman..."

Step Two: Turn back to the page in your journal you labeled, "Clues about my vision," and spend a few minutes reading what you have written there. Now, knowing your vision describes the perfect world as you see it, fill in the blank in the following phrase with the word or words that describes the kind of world you see:

"...I see a world _____."

Step Three: Turn back to the page in your journal you labeled, "Clues about how I am to serve in the world," and spend a few minutes reading what you have written there. Now, complete the following phrase by filling in the blank with the word or words that describes who or what you are to serve in the world:

"I serve _____."

Step Four: Now, we'll pull it all together into your soul name. Combine the results of the work you have just completed in Steps One-Three by putting it together in the following form:

145

"I am a _____ man/woman who sees _____ for _____."

The first blank is from Step One, the second blank is from Step Two, and the third blank is from Step Three.

An example of a completed one might look something like the following:

"I am an open-hearted and loving woman who sees a world at peace for all the children of today and tomorrow."

This is your soul name.

Continue working with various versions of this until you find one that really speaks to you. Feel free to modify the form used here if you need to. You will know you have found your soul name by the strength of the emotional response it elicits when you say it out loud.

3. Plan to spend an entire day walking in nature asking the land and the creatures you meet there for guidance on your vision, your purpose, and your place of service.

When you arrive at the location where you intend to spend your day, create a portal. Use the information in this chapter and your imagination to do so.

Begin your time by standing at the portal and speaking your soul name. Then, ask the land for permission to cross the portal before stepping in.

Chapter 5: The Threshold

Take your journal and record anything that happens during your time in nature.

If you are unable to get out in nature, do this activity in an art gallery or library. Look for guidance from the works of art or the books that catch your attention.

At the end of your time, go back to the portal you crossed when entering the threshold and speak your soul name again.

Cross back over the portal, give thanks to the space that supported you on your journey, and close the portal in a ceremonial fashion.

Later, spend time reflecting on your threshold experience and record your thoughts in your journal.

For additional resources, including free downloadable worksheets you might find helpful in completing these activities, please visit www.liveamythiclife.com.

Chapter 6

Incorporation

Bringing the boon to our people

To complete the cycle, the hero returns from the threshold, bringing with him the boon for his people. Now, the real challenge begins.

> *If you follow your bliss, you put yourself on a kind of track that has been there all the while, waiting for you, and the life that you ought to be living is the one you are living. Wherever you are—if you are following your bliss, you are enjoying that refreshment, that life within you, all the time.*
>
> *- Joseph Campbell*
>
> *Your work is to discover your work, and then with all your heart to give yourself to it.*
>
> *- Buddha*

THE CALLING

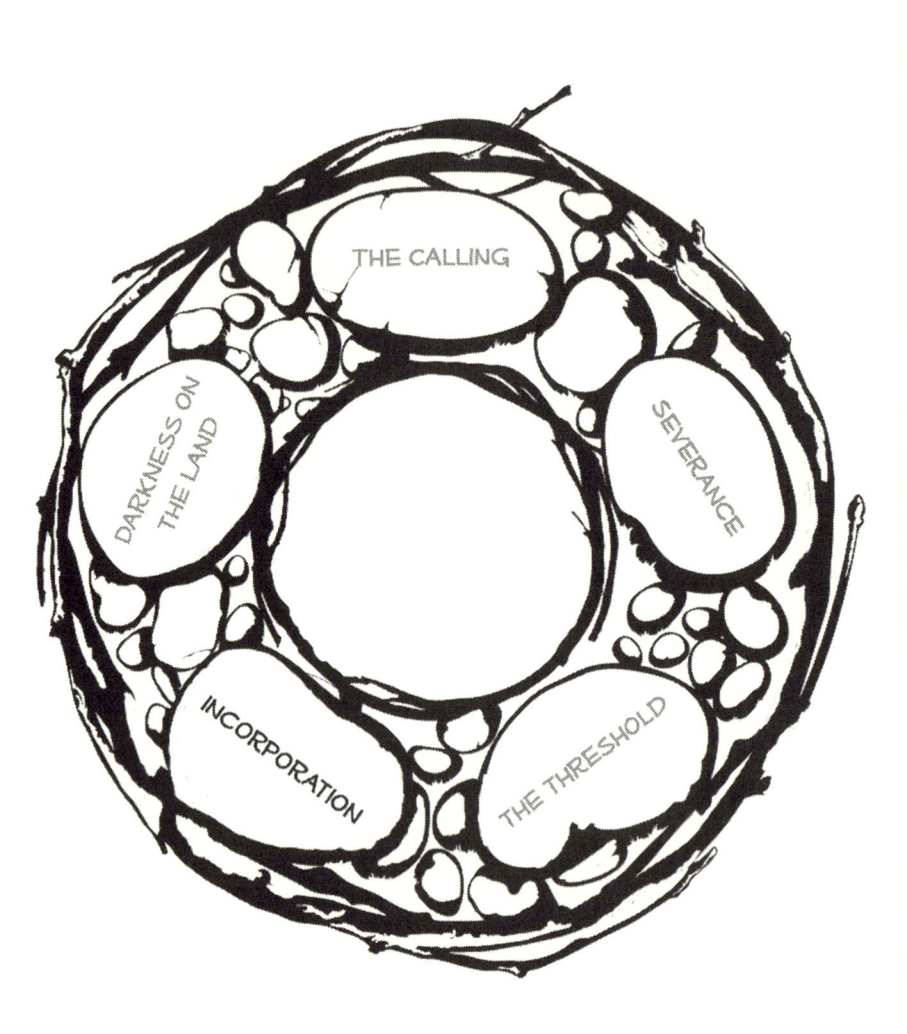

SEVERANCE

THE THRESHOLD

INCORPORATION

DARKNESS ON THE LAND

Chapter 6

Letter from Home: So, you're on your way home. That could be interpreted a couple of ways. Maybe much has been revealed—or nothing. Maybe you have stretched and gone through fire—or not. Maybe you were strong, brave, and courageous—or not. No matter what did or did not happen, I know you have been changed at depth by this process and your soul thanks you. We have come this far together. I will hold you and whatever you come back with in my arms and embrace it all.

Leaving the Wilderness

When I returned to base camp, I began the long process of returning home. Over the next day and a half, my companions and I sat in council and told our stories while the guides reflected them back to us, helping us ferret out their greater meaning. Through this mirroring process, parts of our stories that seemed to be only minor details were viewed in a different light. The mundane turned to magnificent, and our experiences gradually became our personal myths.

On the second day after returning from our solos, we packed up and headed out of the wilderness. On the way back into the Owens Valley, we stopped at the visitor's center at the Ancient Bristlecone Pine Forest to fix lunch. Seeking a moment of solitude, I hiked the trail leading from the parking lot up a steep slope into the very midst of these wise old teachers and sat at the base of a huge one, surrounded by its roots and trunk like enfolding arms.

I had learned about the bristlecones before coming on this trip and was looking forward to finally seeing them. The bristlecone pine trees are the oldest living organisms on earth. Some of them are believed to be over four thousand years old. These trees were saplings when the great pyramids were built. They were already ancient when Jesus walked the streets of Palestine. The bristlecone have been silent witnesses to what we call the period of written history.

The bristlecones have survived for millennia because they grow very slowly, digging their roots deep into the rock and soil and utilizing every bit of the little water and nutrients they can coax out of a very tough environment. Interestingly, some of the oldest of the bristlecones are found in areas that have the harshest of conditions—just below the tree line on north-facing slopes where they receive the brunt of brutal northwest winter winds. They seem to be telling us there is value in adversity. Before Goethe was born, they were already living examples of his wisdom: "That which does not kill us makes us stronger."

The bristlecones, like so many other living organisms on this amazing planet, are perfectly suited to their world. They have lived so long by adapting to a harsh and difficult environment. Any higher in elevation and they would die from thin air; any lower and they would not experience the challenges of nature that have pushed them to thrive for so many years.

As I sat next to the tree and looked out over the Owens Valley toward the Sierra Range in the west, it was hard for me to imagine a more beautiful scene or one filled with a deeper sense of peace. I thought about my new friend and wondered about the span of time he had been standing there. What wisdom was locked within the fibers of this being?

I have often since thought about how we are not that different from the bristlecone pine. Our yearning calls us to find our place of belonging, the place in the world where we are a perfect fit. Like the bristlecone, we will thrive only when we live at the very edge of possibility, becoming one with the environment around us.

We drove the rest of the way down into the Owens Valley and spent the last night camped near a hot spring. That night I lay on the ground looking up at the stars and thought about Peacemaker. What was that all about? What was I to do with that when I returned home? I fell asleep to the sound of coyotes yipping and howling in the hills around me.

I awoke the next morning feeling truly alive. I felt there was nothing I couldn't do with my life and at the same time nothing needed to be done. Everything was important and nothing was. I felt I could die and all would be well. We gathered for our final council and said tearful goodbyes. Somehow, I knew my work with the vision quest was only beginning.

On my way back to Reno, Nevada, where I would catch a flight home the next morning, I drove through the mountain town I had stopped into for coffee the week before. Although it had only been seven days, it felt like a lifetime had passed since my encounter with the pipe. I walked into the store, and the same woman was working there. She looked up, smiling at me in recognition. "I guess it haunted you," she said. "More than you can believe," I replied. I bought the pipe, along with a handmade arrow for my son and a dream catcher for my daughter.

It took several weeks for me to acclimate to home once I returned. It felt as if my heart had been cracked open. Everything

I encountered, everything I experienced, seemed to have a newfound level of significance. I tried to explain to the people who loved me what had happened, and although they could tell something had shifted in me, no one really understood. How could they? They had not been there. They hadn't watched as the stars circled overhead, felt the sunrise on their face after a long cold night alone, or shared in the councils. While I understood the gifts I had discovered and returned with were not for me alone, it was still my personal journey, and no one else could walk it with me.

I began to do some research about Peacemaker and what that might mean in my life. I found an organization working in conflict resolution and volunteered. Although the cause was a good one, something about the work just didn't feel right for me, and I backed away after a few months.

Then, I began to do some research about the pipe and its true purpose and meaning. I found out my idea of the pipe being a "peace pipe" was not accurate. The pipe was a tool for connecting to the Great Spirit that resides in all things. It was therefore, a symbol for oneness and connection, not to signify a treaty had been reached, as I had mistakenly believed. Perhaps Peacemaker had a meaning other than the one I originally gave it.

As I reflect back on the way Peacemaker was revealed to me, I often think about how coyote kept trying to tell me not to take it too literally. He crossed the road right after Peacemaker came into my awareness, howled at me just before sunrise on the last night of my solo, and sang me to sleep on my way home in the Owens Valley as he tried, one last time, to get me to hold my vision lightly.

Some would say coyotes are common in the wild, and it was not unusual to encounter so many of them, but coyote is significant to my journey not because he showed up but because I noticed him and connected him with my searching. Reflecting back, I have come to understand how I could use a little "coyote medicine" in my life. I have learned soul teaches us that way, revealing just enough to get our attention and then inviting us to explore for ourselves.

The greatest gift I received from my vision quest actually came to me through my wife. We were talking one day in the year following my quest when she said to me: "I have always loved the man you are, but I really love the man you are becoming." I needed no further confirmation my journey was worth taking and I had truly returned home.

A little over a year later, I attended a retreat in the Blue Ridge Mountains of Virginia. There, during another threshold experience, I entered into a conversation with a very old oak tree who replied with this question when I asked him for guidance about Peacemaker:

> *What would it take to become the kind of man in whose presence the builders of fences arose of their own accord and began to take them down?*

I knew in that moment I had discovered a question I could live by. Like a Zen koan, I could contemplate this for the rest of my life and never find its final answer. This was a path that would bring Peacemaker into the world, by first allowing him into my heart.

The Return

To incorporate means to give material form to, to embody, to manifest, and to make comprehensible. The incorporation period is, therefore, the time when we attempt to give form to the formless experiences, images, and messages of the threshold time. Now is the time to come back into our bodies so we might begin to bring our vision and purpose into manifestation in service to ourselves and the world.

After hearing and answering the call, doing the severance work, and making the journey into the threshold, many may fail to make the return journey home. This transition from threshold to incorporation can sometimes be a difficult one. Stripped bare by the process of severance and still basking in the glow of threshold magic, it can be a difficult and daunting thing to go back to the world we left behind. It is easy to become enamored of the mystery of the experience and never make the transition into the incorporation phase. The experience itself becomes the thing we build our lives around, rather than the manifestation of the boon in the world to serve our people.

The myths tell of those who don't come home. Joseph Campbell calls this the "refusal of the return,"[1] and it shows up in the myths when the hero chooses to stay in the underworld rather than return with his boon to his people. Sometimes they fall into a deep sleep or decide they are much more comfortable in this land of dreams than they ever were in the world of toil and struggle. Sometimes others must be sent into the underworld to retrieve the hero, setting up yet another round of adventures.

As important as dreaming is, there comes a time to wake up and make our dreams real. Simply having the vision isn't enough; it must be demonstrated and brought to life. The hero must return for the hero's journey to be complete.

Chapter 6: Incorporation

Dragons at the Gate

After all the fear of entering the threshold, all the battles fought there, why would anyone want to stay? There are at least three possibilities, and I call these the Dragons at the Gate. These dragons stand watch at the gate between the threshold and the rest of our lives, just as other dragons guarded the way in. These dragons are closely related, in fact, to the ones we have already faced at the beginning of our journey and are no less fearsome. But, like all dragons, they can be defeated if we have the right weapons.

The first dragon is called Not Enough. Sometimes this dragon guards the portal into the threshold, telling us we are not yet ready for our journey. When it is time to return to our lives, it tells us our work in the threshold is not yet complete. This dragon warns us there is more to be accomplished before we can return to our people and to do so now, as ill-prepared as we are, will result in certain failure and humiliation. There are more lessons for us to learn, he warns. Stay awhile and prepare some more.

Even when there has been a great revelation, the temptation may still be present to continue the search for another one. Our human minds may not be ready to believe what our hearts already know, so we continue to question the messages we have received, discounting them as imaginary and looking outside ourselves for more proof. The jewel is hidden in plain sight, but we continue to turn over stones expecting the answers to be found there. We look for a burning bush, all the while ignoring the whispering wind blowing past the ear, calling our one true name and giving us the question we are to live by.

Your Place in the World

Is there a possible pattern here? Are we attempting to collect spiritually awakening experiences the same way some of us collect material possessions? Sometimes we can get so caught up in our goals-based, success-driven stories, we don't know when to say "enough." Knowing what constitutes enough seems, at times, to be an affliction of those of us who live in the developed world. In the race to accumulate things and experiences, we miss the opportunity to savor even the so-called small moments, the quiet gifts that creep into our lives unnoticed.

There is a balance to be found here, just as there is a balance needed in all areas of our lives. If we rush through the threshold trying to collect as many breakthrough moments as possible, we will miss the richness of each experience. Are we missing the beauty of the sunset as we anticipate the coming sunrise? Are we ignoring the message of the ant working in the sand at our feet while our eyes are transfixed on an empty sky, hoping to see an eagle or a hawk? "Yes, I have the message from the tree and the rock, but I was really expecting to be taught by a mountain on this journey, so I must not be done yet."

We cannot plan for spiritual experiences. Yes, we can do the inner work we need to do. We can work through the process of severance and recognize we are stepping into the threshold. Ultimately, however, there comes a time when we have to let go of our personal control over outcomes and simply allow what will be to be.

I had that kind of experience standing in the gift shop holding the pipe for the first time. I received a lifetime's worth of messages in that one moment, and still, it wasn't enough for me. The rest of the trip was life changing, but it is the message from the symbol of the pipe that has continued to teach me. For me, the pipe is the onion I keep pealing back one thin layer at a time. The pipe I brought home is only an object; its power for me is in its meaning of connection, community, and service. Yet, I also remember how quickly I wanted to move along to what I thought was my true quest.

We also need a sense of worthiness. We must feel worthy of the gifts we discover. We must realize that we can only recognize the beauty and wisdom we experience if we contain them within us. Remember the advice from the woman in the gift shop? She said, "If it haunts you, you will know that it's yours." The yearning that drew us into this experience emanates from the boon we already possess.

We were called into the threshold by a yearning of our souls; we will know our time there is done when we yearn to return home. We can conquer the dragon called Not Enough by following the yearning and by knowing when to say "good enough." We are never entirely prepared for the road ahead, just as we weren't entirely prepared for the road just walked. Our job is the same now as it was at the start of our journey: to listen for the still, small voice inside and follow it home.

The second dragon we may encounter on the way home is called Seduction. This dragon tells us the threshold is preferable to our daily lives. He whispers in our ear our vision is a precious thing but one that will not survive in the light of day. Better to stay and worship the vision itself than to carry it home where it will quickly dissolve into nothing more than a memory. Those who fall prey to this dragon spend an eternity polishing and shining their vision until it gleams like gold, but they never take the vision home to their people.

The seductive power the threshold has over us might make it difficult to return home. This is particularly true if we have had powerful experiences there. The threshold, whether experienced figuratively and metaphorically while going about our normal routines or by going on a physical journey like a vision quest, can be a place of magical power that, once experienced, exerts a magnetic pull on us.

The threshold is a place where anything is possible. We are very powerful in this place of the gods, perhaps not unlike gods ourselves, and the prospect of returning to the physical world, with its limitations of time and space, lacks appeal. Better, we might think, to stay in this space of all-possibility rather than return to a world of challenge and potential failure.

But in order for the cycle to be complete, in order for the journey to truly be heroic, the hero must return from the underworld. He must bring the boon into the world. Without this final step, the entire experience has little meaning. Without the return, the journey is nothing more than a narcissistic exercise in futility, serving no one, not even the hero.

Black Elk, the Oglala Sioux leader, said this:

> *A man who has a vision is not able to use the power of it until after he has performed the vision on earth for the people to see.*[2]

If we stay in the threshold, holding onto our vision like a precious jewel that must be hidden away and protected from the world, we are not only depriving the world of its beauty, but we are also doing a disservice to ourselves. Eventually, the power of the vision can become a burden to carry. We must bring the vision to the light, release it into the world, and then watch as it grows and takes on a life of its own. We can be inspired by the vision, we can choose to live our lives by it, and we can become it, but first we must give it birth by bringing it home.

We all have stories to tell, but will we build our lives around our stories or around the deeper lessons we have learned from them? Will we identify with the journey itself, the wounds and the triumphs, or will we take the lessons those wounds and triumphs have taught us about ourselves out into the world so others may learn from our experiences? As Black Elk counseled, the power of the vision is birthed through its demonstration. We conquer the dragon called Seduction by remembering why we started our journey. We were called to find something lost or stolen and to return it to our world so our people might live.

The third dragon we might meet is called Fear. He has long been with us and carries the secret weapon of humiliation. This dragon is perhaps the fiercest of all. We might have faced him on our way into the threshold. He seems to follow us wherever we go, no matter what phase of life we're in.

We have changed since our departure. Will our friends and family accept us on our return? Will they like the new person standing before them, or are they too deeply invested in the old one we left behind to even notice or recognize a change has taken place? Will our old world still belong to us, or will we be outcasts, strangers in our own land? Perhaps it would be best to stay hidden away in the darkness than to risk not being accepted on our return.

Sometimes giving can be the hardest thing we do. What is it we are to give? To whom do we give it? Will our gift be appreciated? Will it be accepted? What good can we do, anyway? These questions and concerns can keep us stuck where we are, our gift slowly burning in our soul with no discernable way out into the world.

The simple answer is to just keep showing up and giving our gifts as authentically as we can in every moment we can.

The more we do that, the more people we touch. The more we do that, the more deeply developed our gift becomes. We serve ourselves as we serve the world. What a beautiful concept!

Perhaps the greatest fear we face, however, is not failure or rejection but the fear of success. While that might seem odd, it is true for many people. Our egos become so attached to the form our life has taken, fear rattles its saber at the first hint of change. While the language ego uses sounds like, "Don't try that, you might fail," in truth, it is saying, "Don't try that, you might succeed—then where will I be?" Sometimes, we fear having it too good—having all our dreams come true—more than we fear failing at them.

Why would success be something we fear? Perhaps, again, it's a lack of feeling worthy. Many of us believe we are not worthy of having the life of our dreams. We have been taught life is all about struggle, we live in a universe of scarcity, rather than abundance, and there is only so much joy to go around. Others see life as endless competition and the only way to get ahead is to do so at the expense of someone else.

Here is the truth we need to know to slay the dragon called Fear: We live in an abundant universe filled with limitless possibilities. Not only are all the resources needed to support our soul's desires available to us and ready to be deployed, but the universe actually needs for this to happen. The universe needs us to complete it. Do not believe you are not worthy of your dreams. If you can dream it, not only can you become it, you already *are* it. The only thing remaining is to claim it.

Do not allow the fear of failure or the fear of success to keep you stuck in the threshold. Don't be seduced into staying there by the power of the place itself. You are more than enough, and you are called to boldly bring your vision to your people, even if your people have not yet shown up. They are out there, and they are waiting for you. As you begin to express your vision and serve your greater purpose, the people and the causes you are to serve will show up in your life. You become a powerful attracting force when you live from a place of vision and purpose, so you can rest assured those who need your gifts, as well as those meant to assist you and work with you in fulfilling your vision, will appear at the right time, in the right manner.

Actually, all three of these dragons, as well as any others we might face within our minds, are only manifestations of the ego, guises the ego takes on in order to maintain its control over us. If we are ever to transcend the power of the ego, we have to align ourselves with something bigger and more powerful. This is the gift of a compelling vision and purpose rooted in the energy of service. When we fully grasp our hero's boon, the ego may speak, but we will know its voice and will know not to listen.

Once the hero grasps the boon, there really is no choice—he *must* carry it home to his people, because along with the blessing comes a responsibility. The hero now has something of great value, something that will do great good in the world, and there is no other choice to be made.

> ***Reflection question:*** *What dragons seem to be present for you right now as you contemplate bringing your vision and purpose into embodiment? What do you think you might say to these dragons to get them to back away?*

Bringing the Boon Home

Once we have committed to bringing our boon into the world, how do we do that? How do we translate those mystical and often confusing threshold messages into reality? In this regard, you may take a clue from my approach on returning from my vision quest and do exactly the opposite. With a poorly articulated vision, I went straight to action steps with the hope, through the activity of moving forward, the vision would become clearer. There is nothing wrong with this approach; after all it is just another kind of journey. But in hindsight I can now see I had the process reversed. We can save ourselves time and effort by becoming clearer at this point about our hero's boon of vision, purpose, and service before moving toward action.

Our soul name is the articulation of our hero's boon. For the purposes of discussion, let's assume our soul name is as follows:

> *I am a vibrant, joy-filled, and playful man who sees a world filled with music so all the children learn to sing their song.*

One way to start the process is to view your soul name like a new pair of shoes. Before you commit to keeping it, try it on and see how it fits. Look at yourself in the mirror and say your soul name out loud. Does it feel like a good fit? Can you see at least a little bit of that person in your eyes when you say your name? Once you are feeling pretty sure about the fit, it's time to take your soul name to the next level by making a commitment to it.

Let's begin with the purpose part of the example soul name. Imagine what it might be and feel like to be a "vibrant, joy-filled, and playful" man. How would this person show up in the world? What kind of activities would he be drawn toward? What kind of people would he associate with? How would he react to all the little challenges that present themselves through the course of the day? What kind of clothes would he wear? What would his home look like?

The more we try on this idea, the more we will begin to realize we are not putting on something new; we are allowing that which has always been within us to emerge. We are like the butterfly breaking out of the cocoon. The butterfly was always there, even as it lived within the skin of the caterpillar. The vibrant, joy-filled, and playful man was always there within us, as well. The more we see ourselves in this new way, the more we will come to know it is true. The more we know it is true, the more we will begin to show up in the world as that person.

There is inherent in this process the continuation of the severance. The more time we spend being a vibrant, joy-filled, and playful man, the more we will come to see where in our lives we are incongruent with this idea. As we identify those places of incongruence, we can then begin to let them go, perhaps in a severance ceremony like we used before entering the threshold. Little by little, we will peel away the old layers revealing more and more of our true nature.

If we find this process difficult, we can remember the image of the butterfly emerging from its cocoon. In its struggle, the butterfly develops the strength it will need to eventually spread its wings and fly. In our process, we may also struggle to break completely free from the cocoon of our old self, but it is through our struggles that we develop the strength to fully and completely accept this new person we are coming to know.

Now, let's begin to imagine what "a world filled with music" might look like (or, in this case, sound like). If our vision is a world filled with music, then we will begin to find evidence everywhere this is true. As we begin to find small examples of the truth of our vision, our minds will become more open to the possibility of even greater manifestations of our vision. We will begin to notice not just the music playing over the stereo system in the coffee shop but also the rhythms of the rain on the window and the sound of car tires on the pavement. As we have more of these experiences, we will develop a deeper level of faith that our vision is not only possible, but also necessary.

The process of manifesting our vision will have its own accompanying form of severance. The more we come to see our vision in the world, the more we will notice those parts of our lives not in alignment with it. Have we been stifling our own voice as we try to see a world filled with music? Do we participate in activities that support this vision or hinder it? Does the kind of work we do or the environment we do it in fit this vision? Gradually, we can begin to make choices about our lives using our vision to guide us.

This brings us to the part of our name that identifies who or what we are to serve in the world. Service is more about a commitment to a way of life than it is about taking particular steps toward a goal. In this context, service is not just showing up once a month to volunteer at a soup kitchen, as important as such acts of kindness are; it is about living every moment connected to an idea too big to be fully contained in one person.

Let's return again to the soul name example we have been using. If the way we are to express the idea of service is by helping "all the children to learn to sing their song," we could begin by volunteering to help organize a children's choir at our church or by teaching music to kids at a local day care. Either of these choices would be a great way to express our vision and purpose. We could also look at this a bit more broadly and less literally. How do we define "all the children?" Is it all the children in our neighborhood, city, or state, or is it every child on the planet? And what exactly does our soul mean by "sing their song"? It could simply mean we are to teach children to sing, but what gift will the children receive by learning to sing? While they are developing a love of music, perhaps they also find a new level of self confidence, creativity, or a deeper appreciation for beauty in general? What ripples in the world will be created by those particular gifts?

As you begin to try on your soul name, remember that soul doesn't use literal language; it speaks in metaphor. Look for the bigger idea behind the words you have used. Looked at this way, "sing their song" begins to take on a variety of meanings and, in turn, leads to a myriad of ways to serve in the world.

This example demonstrates some of the power of the hero's boon. We get a glimpse of the kind of world we want to live in (one filled with music, in this example). We find the way we are to bring that vision into form (by being vibrant, joy-filled, and playful). We tie it together through the energy of service to others (all the children singing their song), and lives are changed. We are changed. The world is changed.

As your boon takes form, you can use it to determine what you will allow into your life and what you won't. It becomes a kind of litmus test, a measuring tool by which you can determine the right fit in your relationships, your work, your volunteer activities, your spiritual community. You went to great effort in the severance process to strip away that which was no longer serving you. Now, begin to use your boon to determine what you allow into your life.

Before saying yes to a new relationship with someone, spend some time asking this person about their vision for the world. Before taking on a new responsibility, ask yourself if it will allow your true purpose to come forth. Before agreeing to serve in some manner, ask yourself if this is what you were born to serve. While everything about your life doesn't necessarily have to be an exact fit, there is great value in at least checking for congruence.

If you are still not sure about your soul name and all it implies, try to imagine what it would be like *not* to bring this vision, purpose, and service into the world. When you do so, do you feel a deep sense of loss or grief? Return to spending time with your soul name and then note how that feels. Keep doing this process, making modifications to your soul name until you are clear you have found the one unique name you were born to embody.

As you spend more and more time with this new way of living, continue to look for those parts of your life that do not support this new idea. Consider adding a regular severance ceremony to your practices, perhaps once a month to start, then moving to once a year. The coming of a new year and the ending of the old supports this kind of activity. A regular house cleaning assists you in staying focused on the direction you want to move in and helps free you from distractions.

> **Reflection question:** *Pull out the "Maybe List" you created in Chapter 4. How do you feel about each of the items on your Maybe List at this point on your journey? Begin to circle the items you are now clear you are ready to release. Keep coming back to your Maybe List as you work your way through the rest of this chapter and continue to circle any other items you are ready to release. Add anything else you are now ready to release, as well.*

Creating Forms

You might be tempted, as I was, to rush quickly to the creation of forms once you have found your boon, but I recommend you take some time in doing so. The creation of forms will require time and energy, and it might also involve other people, so you will want to be clear about your boon before beginning this phase. Only after you have spent sufficient time trying on your soul name and doing additional severance work that might arise along the way will you be ready to bring it fully into the world. You will know you are ready when you feel a deep and constant resonance in your heart each time you speak your soul name aloud. Once you are ready, there are two general forms you will create: intentions and action steps.

Intentions

An intention is a statement, spoken or written, about something we want to manifest. When we create intentions, we word them from the perspective that they are already done. An intention statement does not ask for something to occur, it assumes it already has. They are statements of what *is* rather than what *could be*—affirmations of reality rather than expressions of hope. Intentions inspire us to move forward. They should be measurable in some way so we will know when we have achieved them, but they are not the action steps themselves; those will come later. Intentions are an attracting force; they attract not only the outcomes being affirmed but also the people and resources needed to make those outcomes real. Here is an example of an intention that might be created from the soul name example we have been using:

> *I am the director of a music program that brings children together from all over the city so they might find their true inner voice.*

Our intentions are seeds planted in the fertile soil of the imagination that grow into manifest outcomes in the world. By setting intentions, we create the vehicle that brings our boon into reality. Stating intentions releases the energy that transforms belief into being. They are inspirational statements of specific outcomes, yet are broad enough to allow for bending and flexing as we go. A powerful intention allows for the possibility, perhaps even probability, that what actually manifests is even greater than what we originally imagined.

Action Steps

Once we have created our intentions, the next step is to create action steps that lead to their fulfillment. Action steps don't have to be complicated. Some of them might only require a single step. Others might have multiple parts and take years to accomplish. In either case, they are clear, and it is easy to ascertain when they are complete. Here are some examples of different types of action steps:

> *Call my friend Sam to ask him about the project he is working on with children in the inner city. (One step)*
> *Do an Internet search to see what other programs exist for children in my area. (One step)*
> *Research the various organizations in the area that are doing children's music programs and contact the ones I feel drawn to. (Multi-step)*
> *Create a curriculum of children's music I can offer to local after-school programs. (Multi-step)*

Without action steps, our vision remains just a dream, our purpose is wasted, and those we are meant to serve don't receive our blessing. We need to create and then take action steps if we ever want the yearning to go away.

Before we move on, I would like to make one final comment about intentions and action steps. There was a time in my life when I relished making plans. The linear, left-brained part of me insisted on knowing what the immediate, intermediate, and long term goals and objectives were for any project I undertook. Then, I would establish strategies, action plans, and bench marks for everything.

Just notice, how different this way of creating forms is from the soul-directed methods of discovery we have been discussing. If we try to look too far down the road, we can get overwhelmed to the point we don't even start. I am now a big believer in the value of taking small steps and then allowing the results of those steps to guide me in taking the next one. I find I am often reflecting on the story from my childhood of walking on the stones in the river. Each stone needed for the next step appeared as I committed to stepping on the one in front of me.

In the interest of full disclosure, I should tell you I often fell into the river and got wet up to my knees! When I slipped, I would simply climb out of the water and return to the last safe stone I had stepped on to rethink where I should go next. We all slip from time to time and can expect to make mistakes in the process of bringing our hero's boon into the world. When we do, we can always return to our own version of a safe place—our soul name. Keep asking, for example: "What next step would I take as a man who is vibrant, joy-filled, and playful and who sees a world filled with music so all children learn to sing their song?"

So set intentions, but not too many. Create action steps, but just a few. Then, allow the energy of your hero's boon to pull you forward and guide you as you take one step after another. Before long, you will look back and be amazed at just how far you have come.

Practices

As you begin to tease out the pieces of this puzzle, it will be helpful to create regular practices that reconnect you with your time in the threshold. If spending time in nature was a part of your threshold experience, then returning to natural settings on a regular basis will help keep you connected with your boon. If music or some other art form inspired you during your search, then continue to use those forms on a regular basis to keep the boon fresh and alive in your conscious awareness. Continue using the tool of journaling if it was helpful to you.

It is also a good idea to regularly speak your soul name aloud. If the right situation presents itself, try introducing yourself to someone you don't know by using your soul name. That might prove to be a really interesting conversation starter!

You will know you are making progress when you begin to feel as if you are experiencing life from the perspective of the person your soul name describes—when you are seeing the world through the eyes of your vision, making choices from the perspective of your purpose, and waking up each day knowing you are in service to something bigger than yourself. Take time regularly to reflect on your vision and purpose. Do they continue to resonate in your heart? When you hear them, do they hum for you? If not, then you are not there yet. Go back to your threshold, either in your imagination or perhaps physically, and spend time asking for more information. Then return to the processes outlined in this book to see what additional insights you receive. It might take several times through all three stages—severance, threshold, and incorporation—before you finally come to the place where you know that you know that you know.

As you develop intentions, spend time imagining they have come to be. Close your eyes and see them done. See the results of your purpose by seeing the intentions as if they are complete.

Who has been positively affected by them? How are your life and the lives of others better because of the manifestation of this intention? If you don't feel a sense of excitement and deep inner joy from doing this, then you don't have the right intention. In this process, you are looking for a sense that this is not only a *good* thing to do, but it is also *your* thing to do. Ask not just if you *could* do it, but ask rather if you *should* do it.

When you work on your action steps, see yourself doing them. Do you feel joy at the thought of doing these things? Are you doing them in the way, through the mediums, and in the environment that feels right for you? Does there seem to be a fit between the action steps and your gifts and desires? Do you get a sense you were born to do these things?

Although you might feel fear at the thought of some of your action steps, don't confuse the fear with a message the step is not yours to do. Fear can and should be worked through because it is a great teacher, but experiencing fear is not the same thing as looking at an action step and knowing it is not a match to your gifts. If an action step is clearly a necessary part of manifesting an intention, but you are also clear it is not yours to do, it might be you are not the person to complete this particular step. Perhaps there is another person who is just waiting for the opportunity, and there is a partnership to be formed. Remain open to the possibilities and see what the universe will provide.

There was a time when my wife was putting together a new business that clearly supported her vision for the world. It was also clear to her the business she was working on was a vehicle to fulfilling her purpose. She set an intention that had an action step that included a sales function. At this point, she felt stopped cold. She didn't have much experience in sales, and although she was not afraid of doing it, she knew it just wasn't hers to do. In addition, spending time making sales calls would take her away from those components of the business that called to her in the first place and she was very clear were hers to do. Rather than giving up, she opened up. Within weeks of speaking her need, an individual with tremendous sales skills, experience, and contacts appeared in her life. Not only was this person skilled, she also shared my wife's vision for the world. They formed a partnership, and the project moved forward. That's how it works. Our need is going to be perfectly matched by someone else's desire to give, and our purpose will move forward.

Throughout the incorporation process, there are three additional bits of advice that will serve you well: first, always follow your instincts, allowing your inner guide to direct you as you move through this process. Second, throughout your journey, stay focused on where you want to go without worrying about what the path is supposed to look like. While you can take inspiration from others who have walked similar paths, everyone's journey is unique. Third, do your best to have fun. This process is not about making your life hard; it's about finding your joy.

A New Beginning

The hero returns home to find their people waiting, and we do, as well. But somehow nothing seems the same because *we* are not the same. We might feel not so much changed as turned inside out. Nothing looks the same from this new perspective of the soul, and nothing ever will again.

Your Place in the World

The hero might want to rest awhile, and it is a rest well deserved. But do not rest too long, for there is work to be done. There are visions to be seen, missions to be accomplished, and a life to be lived. The story, as Campbell would tell us, began with an ending and now ends with a new beginning.

Here is to your new beginning. The world is waiting for you.

Chapter 6: Incorporation

Activities

The following activities are designed to help you bring your hero's boon into the world.

If you have difficulty with doing these activities, try rereading the sections in the chapter titled *Bringing the Boon Home* and *Creating Forms*. You might also want to visit www.liveamythiclife.com where you will find worksheets you can download and use for these activities.

1. This activity will help to clear out whatever remains of the "old you" that might prevent the "real you" from coming forth.

    Step One: Take out your severance Maybe List. Spend some more time with any items that have still not been circled. Is there anything else you wish to release? Work with the list until you feel it is good enough for now, remembering you can always repeat this process in the future.

    Step Two: Perform a severance ceremony with any remaining items you are clear need to be released in order to fully embody your vision, purpose, and way of serving in the world. Speak your soul name as a part of the ceremony; knowing this is who you have come to be. Go back and look at Activity 4 at the end of Chapter 4 for some ideas about how you might perform this ceremony.

2. This activity will help you to begin to try on your soul name as described in this chapter in the section, *Bringing the Boon Home*.

Step One: Create reminders around your home about your soul name. Be creative and have fun with this. Here are some suggestions:

- Write your soul name in big letters on a sign that you hang in a prominent place.
- Find pictures in magazines that represent aspects of your soul name and create a colorful collage from them. Hang the collage where you will see it every day.
- Place signs around your home where you will find them regularly.
- Send inspirational cards to yourself addressed to your soul name.
- Add your soul name, or parts of it, to the signature you use on emails you send.

3. This activity will help you to create intentions to support bringing your boon into the world.

Step One: Find a place where you can sit comfortably for at least half an hour without being disturbed. Have your journal and a pen or pencil within reach.

Step Two: Speak your soul name three times, each time with passion and commitment, but getting gradually softer each time you say it. "I am ____. I am ____. I am ____." Close your eyes and speak your soul name once more silently to yourself. Then, take several breaths from deep in your belly.

Step Three: Begin to use your imagination to see yourself at some point in the future.

- Where are you?
- What does it look like?
- What are you doing?
- What does it feel like to be in this place and time doing what you are doing?

Allow your imagination to put you there. Don't just observe it but experience it. Wait and listen.

Step Four: Start to create statements beginning with "I am" that describe what you are observing. Open your eyes when you need to make notes in your journal about these intentions. In this process, you might get one intention or you might get several. You may have to try several times before you get anything. Don't be discouraged. Keep going back until you get at least one intention.

Step Five: Complete this activity by stating your soul name once more, taking a deep breath, and opening your eyes. Spend a few minutes while the memory is still fresh reflecting on this activity. Make additional notes in your journal about what messages you have received.

Step Six: Select the three or four intentions that move you most deeply and use them regularly throughout the day. Create a practice that includes your soul name and your intentions. Some examples:

- Write your intentions on signs and place them around your home where you will see them regularly.

- Start and end each day by saying your soul name and your intentions several times.

- If you have created a collage inspired by your soul name, add additional images that remind you of your intentions.

4. This activity will help you to create action steps that support your intentions.

Step One: Find a place where you can sit comfortably for at least half an hour without being disturbed. Have your journal and a pen or pencil within reach.

Step Two: Speak your soul name three times, each time with passion and commitment, but getting gradually softer each time you say it. "I am ____. I am ____. I am ____." Close your eyes and speak your soul name once more silently to yourself. Then, take several breaths from deep in your belly.

Step Three: Allow one of your intentions to come into your conscious awareness. Silently speak this intention three times. Now, see yourself at a time in the future when this intention has come to be. Begin to ask questions like this:

- What challenges did I overcome to get to where I am today?
- What were the steps I took and strategies I used?

- Who helped me along the way?
- What experiences did I have, what skills did I learn, and what support did I receive to get to where I am today?

Be as specific as you can and take notes in your journal as you receive messages.

Step Four: Use the information you found in Step Three to begin to create action steps for this intention.

Step Five: Repeat this process for each of your intentions.

Hint: Remember for this activity you are asking these questions as if everything you needed to do to bring about the intention has already happened. It very well might be you don't see all the action steps you will take the first time you do this exercise. If you come away with one step each time you do this activity, it will be enough to keep moving forward. Watch for places where one action step or a series of them might help to support more than one intention.

5. Reward yourself. This has been a long journey and you have worked hard. Find some meaningful way to congratulate the hero you are for bringing your gifts to us all.

For additional resources, including free downloadable worksheets you might find helpful in completing these activities, please visit www.liveamythiclife.com.

EPILOGUE: Living the mythic life

Great ideas...come into the world as gently as doves...if we listen attentively, we shall hear, amid the uproar...a faint flutter of wings, the gentle stirring of life and hope. Some say that this hope lies in a nation: others, in a man. I believe rather that it is awakened, revived, nourished by millions of solitary individuals whose deeds and works every day negate...the crudest implications of history. As a result, there shines forth fleetingly the ever threatened truth that each and every one of us, on the foundation of our own sufferings and joys, builds for all.

-Albert Camus

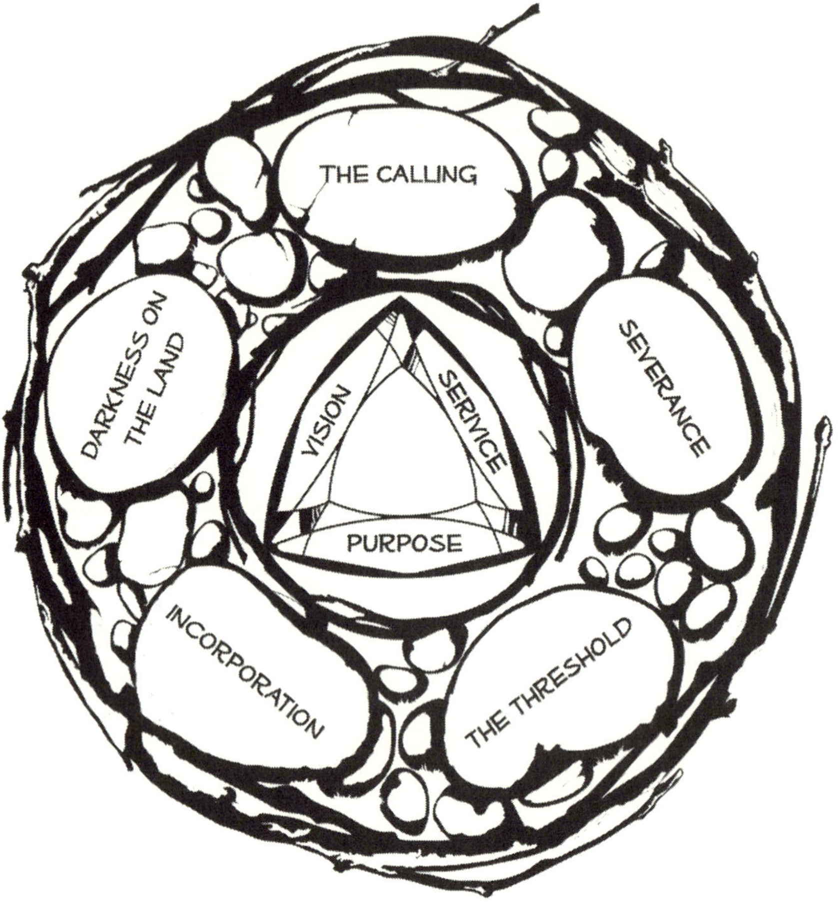
THE CALLING
SEVERANCE
THE THRESHOLD
INCORPORATION
DARKNESS ON THE LAND
VISION
SERVICE
PURPOSE

Epilogue: Living the mythic life

Although some time has passed since I returned from my vision quest, the incorporation continues. It seems I have gotten desert sand in my shoes, desert sky in my eyes, desert wind in my hair, and the mountains in my mind—and I can't get them out.

A few months after returning home, I started journaling about the ideas that would eventually become the book you now hold in your hands. About the same time I decided to begin the training program to become a vision quest guide. I now offer weekend programs, classes, and talks; all in support of my vision of a world alive with vision, purpose, and service. And, I also let my boss know I had to turn down the very attractive offer that was the catalyst starting this whole journey.

A little over a year after my vision quest, I found myself in Death Valley in an apprentice role on another quest. I have many fond memories from the trip, but there was one day in particular I remember well.

I awoke that morning just as the sun was beginning to make its presence known behind the ridge to my left, casting a soft light over the canyon around me. I knew it would be another beautiful November day in Death Valley, and I looked forward to all it held.

I could hear my co-guides, Alison and Michael, beginning to stir. Alison was fiddling with the stove to heat water for tea and cereal, and Michael was moving around his campsite about one hundred yards away. It was so quiet there, and the air was so pure, sound seemed to carry for miles—in spite of one's attempt to move and speak softly.

It was the start of our fourth full day in Death Valley and the third since the rest of the group had left base camp for the three-day solo portion of their vision quest. I was there to learn to be a vision quest guide, and so I stayed behind to help manage base camp, learn all I could from Michael and Alison, and prepare for the return of the participants on the morning after their third day alone.

Managing base camp was a fairly easy proposition. The camp was a one-and-a-half-mile hike up a canyon wash from where we had parked our cars. There was no source of water in the area, so the most important job each day was to hike down to the cars where water was stored and return with as many gallons as we could carry. While the participants were on their solo, Alison, Michael, and I had to make sure we built up a stockpile of filled water containers to serve everyone's needs for the rest of the week. In the desert, nothing is more precious than water, and the participants would be in no shape to hike out to get their own when they returned from fasting for three days. It was up to us to take care of this important task.

The trick was to go early in the morning in order to hike back up the hill before the sun was fully up. Either that or we hiked down in the evening and back in twilight turning to dark. I had done both and much preferred the morning option. My plan that morning was to avoid the heat of the day by hiking down with Michael before breakfast, returning before the sun was high.

The realization the sun would come up with or without my participation got me moving and out of my sleeping bag. I could hear Michael walking down the hill from his site. Soon, we would set off on our task. Alison would be staying behind this morning and promised to have a hearty breakfast of hot oatmeal ready for us when we returned.

As I walked with Michael down the canyon, I can remember feeling free, fully alive, and totally present to the moment. It was a feeling that had been with me since first scouting the area with Alison and Michael several days before. These days in the desert were so different from my life in the city. Normally, my day ran according to the clock and the demands of family, clients, co-workers, and my job. Out here, the natural progression of the sun was my clock. My focus was directed at basic survival issues and supporting the participants as they prepared for their solo time. This activity of service to others coupled with

Epilogue: Living the mythic life

a visceral connection with the beauty of the natural world around us infused me with a sense of joy and peace. I felt more on purpose than at any other time I could remember. There was no place else I could imagine being other than hiking down the canyon.

As we walked, I asked Michael about the vision quest work. We talked about its history, Michael's teachers, and others who had guided before. Much of our conversation over the previous two days had run along these topics. I felt like a kid with a new toy at Christmas—I couldn't get enough of this stuff. After many years of searching, I felt I had finally found a purpose and meaning for my life, a way to serve that used all of my most treasured skills and abilities while allowing me to spend time in the wilderness that spoke so deeply to my heart.

We stopped a moment for a breather and to take in the scene around us. From where we stood, the wide canyon ran downhill for miles toward the bottom of the Death Valley basin. Behind us, Epaulet Peak raised her brooding head and shoulders, watching over base camp and the solo sites of the participants. We could see for miles in several directions. The scene was so amazing my mind had a difficult time believing it was real. It reminded me of a painted landscape backdrop from an old Hollywood western. Michael and I stood in silence for a moment, taking it all in.

Finally, I spoke. "You know, Michael, life is a beautiful thing... but it is especially beautiful when we live it mythically."

Michael looked at me and slowly smiled. I saw in his face a man who had walked a heroic journey to soul, and now was bringing his deepest, most treasured gifts to his people. As I looked into Michael's eyes, I caught a glimpse of my reflection, and when I did, I saw the face of another man who had come to understand his soul and the gifts it contained. In that moment, in that reflection, I saw Peacemaker.

After a moment, we turned and continued our walk down the canyon to retrieve the water for our people.

———

Each day of our lives we are presented with opportunities to realize our vision, fulfill our purpose, and serve our people. What haunts us is the call to adventure. What haunts us is the mythic life.

Additional Resources

For additional resources to assist you in taking your own personal hero's journey, please visit www.liveamythiclife.com. In addition to information about where the author will be speaking, conducting classes, and leading workshops and retreats, you will also find instructional downloads. These downloads provide additional ideas beyond those in the activities sections of this book on how you can make the most of the process of severance, threshold, and incorporation.

Please contact the author by using the contact form found at www.liveamythiclife.com if you have any questions, desire additional information, or would like to inquire about his availability to speak to your group or lead a workshop or retreat in your area.

The vision quest the author experienced was facilitated by Michael Bodkin and Linda Sartor with Rites of Passage. Rites of Passage is a non-profit organization whose mission is to re-introduce meaningful rites of passage for people of the modern world, so they may be able to mark and celebrate important life transitions with courage, strength and wisdom. Since their founding in 1977, Rites of Passage has guided thousands of adults and youth from a wide variety of backgrounds, occupations and geographic locations on vision quests, retreats, and training programs. For more information, visit their website: www.ritesofpassagevisionquest.org.

About the Author

Tom Anderson is a writer, inspirational speaker, workshop leader, and vision quest guide whose passion is helping others to discover theirs. His own story parallels those of the people he often serves: a life of outward worldly success while urged by a yearning of the soul to live a life of deeper meaning and purpose. Following insights revealed on his first vision quest experience, Tom has answered the call to bring the teaching he received back to a wider audience. These teachings help people discover their deep souls' callings so they might better serve themselves, their communities, and the world.

Tom lives in Overland Park, Kansas with his wife and their two children.

Notes

PROLOGUE

Epigraph from David Whyte, "Sometimes," in *Everything is Waiting for You* (Langley, WA: Many Rivers Press, 2003), 4–5

INTRODUCTION: *The call to live a mythic life*

[1] M. E. P. Seligman. *Authentic Happiness: Using the New Positive Psychology to Realize Your Potential for Lasting Fulfillment* (New York: Free Press, 2004).

[2] Bill Plotkin. *Soulcraft* (Novato, CA: New World Library, 2003), 214.

[3] Joseph Epes Brown. *The Sacred Pipe-Black Elk's Account of the Rites of the Oglala Sioux* (Norman, OK: University of Oklahoma Press, 1989), 44–46

[4] Joseph Campbell. *The Hero with a Thousand Faces* (Princeton, NJ: Princeton University Press. 1949), 51.

CHAPTER 1 – MYTH AND THE HERO'S JOURNEY: *Seeing our lives as an adventure of discovery*

[1] Joseph Campbell with Bill Moyers. *The Power of Myth* (New York: Anchor Books, 1988). 38–39.

[2] Campbell with Moyers. 48–49.

[3] Joseph Campbell. *The Hero with a Thousand Faces* (Princeton, NJ: Princeton University Press. 1949)

[4] Campbell with Moyers. 157

[5] Freud, Sigmund and Strachey, James. *The Ego and the Id* (New York: W.W. Norton & Company, Inc. 1960), 11

[6] This ceremony was inspired by a talk given by Rev. Patricia Bass at Unity Church of Overland Park. Rev. Bass credits Rachel Naomi Remin, MD. *My Grandfather's Blessings* (New York: The Berkley Publishing Group, a Division of Penguin Putnam, Inc., 2000), 216–217.

CHAPTER 2 – DARKNESS ON THE LAND: *Finding our vision*

[1] Henry David Thoreau. *Walden; or, Life in the Woods* (New York: Dover Publications, 1995), 4.

[2] Joseph M. Marshall, III. *Walking With Grandfather* (Boulder, CO: Sounds True, 2005), 11–13.

[3] Those who are familiar with the concept of Spiral Dynamics will recognize the phases of this "journey through time" I am describing here. While I use different terms to describe them, my "ages" correspond roughly to the stages of human and cultural development first identified by Clare Graves and then further developed by Don Edward Beck and Christopher C. Cowan in their book, S*piral Dynamics: Mastering values, leadership, and change (Malden, MA: Blackwell Publishing Limited, 1996)*

[4] John Naisbitt, *Megatrends* (New York: Warner Book, 1984), 249–250

CHAPTER 3 – THE CALLING: *Finding our purpose*

Chapter epigraph from David Whyte, "The Soul Lives Contented," in *Fire in the Earth* (Langley, Washington: Many Rivers Press, 1992), 31

[1] Joseph Campbell. *The Hero with a Thousand Faces*, 51.

[2] Campbell. 59.

[3] Paul Hawken. *Blessed Unrest—How the Largest Movement in the World Came into Being and Why No One Saw It Coming* (New York: Penguin Group, 2007)

[4] Campbell. 51.

CHAPTER 4 – SEVERANCE: *Serving our people*

Chapter epigraphs are from George M. Lamsa, *The Holy Bible from Ancient Eastern Manuscripts* (Philadelphia: A.J. Holman Company, 1967) Mt 19:24; and David Whyte, from "Sweet Darkness" in *River Flow* (Langley, WA: Many Rivers Press) 348

[1] Jim Collins. *Good to Great: Why Some Companies Make the Leap...and Others Don't* (New York: HarperBusiness, 2001), Chapter 3.

[2] Matthew 5:6, Lamsa

[3] I first learned about the Loyal Soldier from Bill Plotkin in his book *Soulcraft*, 91–96. Plotkin, in turn, credits Morgan Farley and Molly Brown. See Molly Young Brown, *Growing Whole: Self-Realization on an Endangered Planet* (Center City, Minn.: Hazelden, 1993).

CHAPTER 5 – THRESHOLD: *Claiming what has always been*

Chapter epigraph is from David Whyte, *The Heart Aroused. (New York: Doubleday, 1994), 33*

[1] Mary Oliver, from "The Journey," in *Dream Work* (New York: Atlantic Monthly Press, 1986), 38–39

[2] My friend Susan Beck introduced me to the phrase, "Trouble at the Border," which she used when encouraging me to forge ahead with a project on which we were working together. It's a wonderful metaphor for the barriers we create in our own minds between what already exists in the infinite mind of God and its physical manifestation in our lives. Susan gives credit for this phrase to her teacher Maria Nemeth.

CHAPTER 6 – INCORPORATION: *Bringing the boon to our people*

Chapter epigraph is from Joseph Campbell with Bill Moyers. *The Power of Myth*, 113

[1] Joseph Campbell. *Hero with a Thousand Faces*, 193–196.

[2] John G. Neihardt. *Black Elk Speaks-Being the Life Story of a Holy Man of the Oglala Sioux.* (Lincoln, NE: University of Nebraska Press, 1961), 204

Made in the USA
Charleston, SC
16 June 2010